DON CHERRY'S HOCKEY STORIES AND STUFF

DON CHERRY'S HOCKEY STORIES AND STUFF

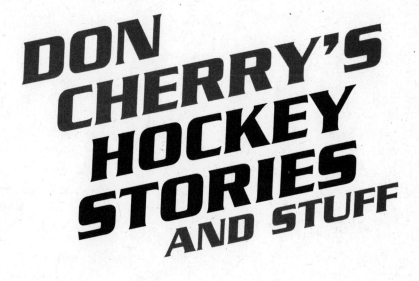

As told to Al Strachan

DOUBLEDAY CANADA

Doubleday Canada and colophon are trademarks

LIBRARY AND ARCHIVES OF CANADA CATALOGUING IN PUBLICATION
Cherry, Don, 1934–
    Don Cherry's hockey stories and stuff / Don Cherry as told to Al Strachan.

Includes index.
ISBN 978-0-385-66674-9

    1. Cherry, Don, 1934–. 2. National Hockey League — Anecdotes.
3. Hockey–Anecdotes. 4. Sportscasters — Canada — Biography. 5. Hockey
coaches — Biography. I. Strachan, Al. II. Title. III. Title: Hockey stories and
stuff.

GV848.5.C53A3 2008   796.962092   C2008-904865-2

For photo credit details please see page 234.

Printed and bound in the USA

Published in Canada by Doubleday Canada,
a division of Random House of Canada Limited

Visit Random House of Canada Limited's website: www.randomhouse.ca

BVG 10 9 8 7 6 5 4 3 2 1

For Mom and Dad

WHEN I WAS ABOUT FIFTEEN OR SIXTEEN, every Saturday I would go fishin' with the guys. It was automatic. It was the thing to do in Kingston. We'd fish in the morning and most of the afternoon, and play ball that night at the cricket field. Life was lovely.

Then one Saturday afternoon, I discovered the *Baseball Game of the Week* on TV with Dizzy Dean, the old St. Louis pitcher, and his partner Buddy Blattner. Then Pee Wee Reese took Buddy's spot.

It was magic, and my days of fishin' on Saturday were over. I never missed Dizzy. I remember he used to get criticized for the way he spoke and acted on TV. When Dizzy thought the game was over, he'd start singing "The Wabash Cannonball."

When Pee Wee Reese asked him one time if he ever tried to break up a double play, he said, "Yeah, and the guy drilled me in the head with the throw to first, knocked me cold and they carried me off on a stretcher. They took X-rays of my head. They found nothin'."

I know other guys have said that, but he really meant it. I tell ya, he used to kill me.

Somebody wrote a book on Dizzy, and it was Dizzy tellin' stories of baseball in his own words. He said things like "slud into third."

Some people did not appreciate his English, but I loved it. It was like Dizzy was sittin' down with me, just tellin' baseball stories.

And that's what I'd like this book to be — just like we were sittin' down, tellin' stories in my own language. I know I'll be criticized, because for some reason people are not too thrilled with the way I speak.

In fact, CBC wanted to fire me my first month on *Hockey Night in Canada*. The brass told my boss, Ralph Mellanby, "This guy is awful. Get him off the air. We owe it to the English-speaking children of Canada."

I stayed because Ralph, who had just won an Emmy or somethin' for the Olympics, said, "If he goes, I go."

But he also said, "I have to admit, Canada is a land of two official languages and Cherry speaks neither." It kinda hurt my feelings.

So don't blame Random House or Al Strachan for the way the book is presented. I wanted the book to be like a couple of guys sittin' down with a few pops tellin' hockey stories.

I hope you enjoy it.

AL'S NOTE: *My job on this book was an easy one. Don told the stories. I transcribed them, collated them and checked a few facts.*

Rather than have a glossary that forces you to flip to the back of the book to see who Don is talking about, we decided to use this method. Don will tell his story and then, if there's a need for it, I'll add some information in one of these notes. Mercifully, they will become fewer in number as the book progresses.

Ralph Mellanby was the executive producer of Hockey Night in Canada *for more than two decades. During his broadcasting career, he won five Emmies and was involved in the telecast of no fewer than twelve Olympic Games. His son, Scott, played in the National Hockey League for twenty-one years. For more information about Ralph, read his book* Walking with Legends: The Real Stories of Hockey Night in Canada.

* * *

To even go farther with a little story—it must have been in 1983, my first year on the CBC doing "Coach's Corner." A producer sat me down the morning of a game, if you can believe it, between the

Islanders and Edmonton, and he said—John Shannon was there, and Dave Hodge, for breakfast and I went down all bubbly and everythin' and ready for the game.

So the producer said in front of these guys, "I'm really worried about the way you pronounce names."

Now, this is six months in! I'd been doing it now for six months and all of a sudden, he tells me the day of the game in the Stanley Cup finals that I don't pronounce Gillies right when I'm talkin' about Clark Gillies! That really bothered me at the time—because it was my first year, I guess.

I used to worry about things like that back then.

So I immediately went upstairs and called a good friend of mine, Gerry Patterson, and I said, "Gerry, you know, I'm a little worried. You know, he gives me this the day of the game."

So Gerry phones Ralph Mellanby and says, "Don's a little worried, the way he pronounces names."

Ralph says, "Aw, let him pronounce the names the way he wants." He says, "That's half his charm."

Well, you should have heard me pronounce the names *that* day! I tell ya, ya couldn't recognize anybody.

So this is the book and this is the way it's going to be. I'm going to mispronounce names and use my English. Any other way and it wouldn't be me.

AL'S NOTE: *In those days, Dave Hodge was with Don on "Coach's Corner." There's more on him later.*

John Shannon was a producer. He had started as a runner, a fancy word for gopher, and had moved steadily up the ladder. He eventually became the executive producer of Hockey Night in Canada *and was generally conceded to be the best hockey producer in the world. As a result, the International Olympic Committee consistently sought his services to produce Olympic hockey telecasts. He's now the NHL's senior vice-president of broadcasting.*

Gerry Patterson was Don's first and only agent and a good friend.

* * *

Every summer, when the free agents get signed, I get asked the same question. Do I resent the players getting the money that they're getting now?

I've got to admit, it has really gone nuts. Can you imagine? Mats Sundin scored 30 goals in the 2007–08 season and he's offered $20 million for two years by Vancouver! He's offered $20 million and he's got to think about it?

That's $10 million a year. Salaries only cover the regular season, so that's $10 million for 82 games. That's $121,951.22 a game. If he plays 20 minutes, that's almost $6100 a minute!

Another guy, Brian Campbell. Good little defencemen. Eight years, $57 million. Good for him. Get it while you can.

I remember back in the sixties, you had six teams, and it was tough to get into the NHL and even get a paycheck, never mind $20 million. The owners said, "Hey, it's a privilege for you to play in the NHL. Here's your salary. Take it or leave it." They got away with it because they had a lot of guys sittin' in the weeds waitin' to take spots.

I figured it out. There were six American Hockey League teams. There were six Central Hockey League teams. Then there was the Western Hockey League. They had six. They were all pro leagues, so add them up and that's 18 teams in minor pro.

Add the NHL teams and there's 24 pro teams.

To get to the 30 teams that they have in the NHL now, they'd have to go way down to the minors and get six teams from an amateur league.

It makes you think, doesn't it?

The pay in the NHL then was brutal. Nobody complained or you were gone.

It was bad in the NHL. But think about how bad it was in the minors. I made $4500 my first year, and in the ninth year, they cut me to $4200 when I went to Three Rivers, Quebec.

My raise came when I went to Rochester. Jack Riley, the general manager, gave me $6000. I was as happy as a pig in mud, and I didn't find out until years later when I was coachin' the Bruins that the only reason that Jack gave it to me was that all the rookies down from the Maple Leafs were earning $6000.

He didn't have the heart to give us confirmed minor-leaguers that had been in the league nine years less than the Leafs' kids were getting.

But to go back to the question. Do I resent the salaries guy are getting now?

Not one bit. I'm a player's guy. Like I said, get it while you can. The players were stiffed for a long time. Guys like Gordie Howe and Rocket Richard never got their just dues and the pension was a joke.

I was a minor-leaguer and I got what I deserved, but these guys were the best players in the world and they got stiffed. Gordie was makin' peanuts when he signed for Jack Adams in Detroit. His signin' bonus was a team jacket! Jack Adams said he looked on Gordie like a son and then he stiffed him.

Bobby Baun, who was traded to Detroit from Toronto, was having breakfast one day with Gordie. Back then nobody ever talked about their salary. Don't ask me why, but they didn't.

But Bobby did and he said to Gordie, "Wake up, I'm making what I'm making and you're making what you're making? C'mon. Smarten up."

Gordie did smarten up. He marched up to see Jack Adams and got paid what he was worth.

Good for your Bobby Baun.

I asked an agent what Bobby Orr would make now. In his last full year, Bobby scored 46 goals, 89 assists and was plus-128. To put that into perspective, the best defenceman in the NHL in 07–08 was Nick Lidstrom in Detroit at plus-40.

The agent said, "Well, when we went into negotiate, after Bobby got part of the club, then we'd talk salary."

As you read this, answer me honestly. If you were offered this kind of money, wouldn't you take it?

The owners wouldn't pay it if they didn't have it. The only problem about all this is that the fans end up taking it in the ear.

* * *

I feel my greatest contribution to hockey in the minors was my idea of keeping the beer cold.

You had to realize that the coach knew there was drinking goin' on at the back of the bus, but you had to sort of hide it and not let on that you were drinking. Don't rub it in.

When he come by to go to the washroom in the back, you had to hide it. But he knew what was goin' on. He knew.

So we had our beer, but the beer was warm. We were wondering how we were gonna keep it cold. I started thinkin', it would be cold if we could get it outside. But how do we get it outside?

You can't go down underneath into the luggage areas and get it. All of a sudden, it hit me. What we do is, we'll get a pillowcase and we'll put six beers in it. Where the card games are, we'll put the pillowcase outside the window, and close the window tight on the pillowcase with the beer in it. It's below zero outside and the beer will be ice cold.

So I bring my pillowcase down from the hotel. I'm sorry to say I stole it, but I have to say I did. So we play the game that night. We are on the bus now, the card game is all set up, and I say, "Okay guys, give me six beer." They thought I was nuts. I said, "Give them to me."

I put them in the pillowcase. I put them outside. We played cards for about twenty minutes. I said, "Hold the cards." I opened the window, pulled the pillowcase in, cracked the beer and they were absolutely ice cold.

The guys all toasted me for the greatest invention since the wheel.

AL'S NOTE: *With the exception of one playoff game for the Boston Bruins in 1955, Don spent his entire playing career in the minors.*

* * *

In 1980, I had just started out doing my banquets. I did them to survive when I finished coaching in Colorado, and I was with Gerry Patterson, and we're driving to Goderich to do a banquet.

I had taken two days to write, like everybody else that goes to these banquets, a speech about the meaning of life and how you must strive, and all that stuff there. So I'm practising it and I've got it all down and I said to Gerry, "I'm going through the meaning of life, you know, like all the rest of the guys do. You have to do this."

And I says, "How do you like that, Gerry?"

He says, "Horsecrap."

I says, "What?"

He says, "Horsecrap." He says, "These people comin' up here, they don't want to hear all that stuff. They wanna hear you. They expect to see you like when you're on 'Coach's Corner.' They don't want to hear the meaning of life. Just go and talk to them in your language."

Gerry is right. They don't want to hear my thoughts on life and how to get better. They just want to hear some stories.

I'm the same guy you see on TV, but I was going to change because I saw everybody else doin' it. I'm the same. Maybe a little flowered-up language or somethin'. That's all.

AL'S NOTE: *You can probably figure out that Gerry Patterson didn't really say "horsecrap." Furthermore, you can probably figure out what he did say.*

But Don wanted this book to be suitable reading for kids, so we've paraphrased some of the profanities. When you see ****, you can assume that someone used a specific four-letter word. If you're an adult, you can probably figure out what it is. If you're a kid, you can probably figure it out as well, but at least you can let your parents think you can't.

* * *

People ask me if I remember my first game coachin' the Boston Bruins. I sure do. It was a disaster.

It was in Buffalo. It was 1973 and the Bruins had been the Stanley Cup champions in 1972. Now this punk from Rochester, a minor-leaguer, was going to show them how to do it. We got hammered 9–5 and I'll never forget a little guy with a bubble helmet got a hat trick. A rookie! Danny Gare. I couldn't believe it. I was in a state of shock. I think the headline was, "Cherry's initial debut as a coach of the Boston Bruins a disaster." That was the headline.

So after the game, I'm sitting on the bus and our goalie Gillie Gilbert is sitting in front of me and he turns to the guy next to him: "Well, that's it for me. My average, from here on in . . . That's it for me."

I thought, "This is my goaltender for the rest of the year?" So Gillie and I never got off to a good start. We went the rest of the year and I think we had close to a hundred points and we played Chicago in the playoffs. It was one of those treacherous two-out-of-three series. We beat them really bad the first game. Really bad. I think it was 7–1 or 8–1. They had headlines in the paper:

"Tony Esposito finished."

"Chicago is finished."

"Esposito looks like a sieve."

"Swiss cheese," they called him.

"Uh oh," I said, "we're in for a tough time now."

Then we go to Chicago and I'll never forget they got an offside goal to win the game. We come back to Boston, two out of three — mind you now — and we pour 58 shots at 'em to 16 — 16 or 18 shots — and they beat us by one goal or two goals and Esposito was unbelievable, I'll tell ya.

He reverted right back to when he was a kid. Anyhow, Gillie let in I forget how many, and he had 16 shots on him and a reporter went to him after the game and said, "Well, you were outshot

58–16. You lost the game. You had 16 shots."

He said, "But out of the 16, there was a lot of hard ones."

The reporter told me, and I says, "But how many hard ones, do you think, was in the 58 we put on Esposito?"

So we never were friends. We never liked each other afterwards.

* * *

Then we got Gerry Cheevers the next year and Cheevers went on a hot streak and I just favoured him. I hate to say what I did to Gillie.

A coach always has an idea that there's a good chance he'll lose, and that's the games I'd give Gillie all the time. If we were goin' into Philly and I knew we weren't ready, or if we had three games in four nights, I'd give him to Philly.

But here's the strange thing. A few years ago, Timothy, my son, was lookin' in the yearbook. Gillie won seventeen straight games, which is a record. And let me tell ya, for him to win seventeen straight games, with the games I gave him, I tell ya boy, that was pretty tough.

But we never did get along.

I remember we had breakaways in practice one time and I went in and tried to deke him and he tripped me on purpose. I went headfirst into the boards. That was a good one—almost killed myself.

But I got up and I said, "Okay."

Bobby Schmautz and all the crazy shooters, I put down at Gillie's end and saved all the good ones for Cheevers.

But can you imagine, seventeen straight games and all the hard ones? So it worked out for him, too.

* * *

At the 2008 All-Star Game, they were doing breakaways and they had no helmets on. You could see all the guys. They were so good-lookin'. It looked so good—the guys goin' in and dekin' and stuff like that and the fans could see them. They could relate.

For instance, Alexander Ovechkin, the guy from Washington. You never see him in the regular games. All you see is a bubble helmet. He's got that tinted glass down to his chin and through the glass you see two little peephole eyes. What a way to sell the game!

I'm not saying go back to no helmets or whatever, but at least let the fans see what the players look like in the All-Star skills competition.

I can always picture Bobby Orr flying down the ice, and Guy Lafleur. Their Montreal uniforms, I swear, their sweaters seemed to be made of silk and he had long blond hair. He'd be flying down there and that sweater would be fluttering in the breeze. It was unbelievable how he looked. It was something to behold.

I know we can't go back to those days, but in the All-Star Game, you'd think somebody would come up with the idea. Let the fans see the players. What the heck's the difference?

Or do it during the shootouts in the regular games. It just doesn't make sense to me. We gotta sell the game.

* * *

No doubt the best salesman the NHL has ever had is Wayne Gretzky. Although I've got to admit, Sidney Crosby is workin' at it too. He does a good job.

When I was in Colorado, Colorado at the time was not thought of very highly as a hockey centre. Teams used to figure, "Oh well, we'll just drop in and grab two points in Denver, then be on our way."

That was before I got there.

A lot of them still grabbed their two points on account of Hardy Astrom, the Swedish Sieve, but they were a little harder to get.

One time I got there early to the game—I'd say it was about 4:30—walking around the corridor underneath the stands, and here comes Gretzky in his underwear. He was walkin' around to go on the five o'clock news on Denver TV.

It's one thing to do television commercials in Toronto and Montreal and New York, but here he was in Denver goin' on TV.

He walked by and just nodded. He was sellin' the game.

* * *

People are always asking me what the heck is goin' on when you're flying all the time? It must really be somethin'.

Well, it does get scary. I think one of the scariest trips we ever had, and we had a lot of them—I'll tell you some more, but this was one of them. We were flying into Chicago from Boston, and we got into Chicago and as they do, they had a great snowstorm there.

Well, you can imagine O'Hare Airport, how it's backed up. So we were out over Lake Michigan and we flew around and around and around, waiting. What made this scary was that a month before that, a plane had circled around and around and had run out of fuel and had crashed in the lake.

Anyhow, we're circling and now we go and we finally get in and we get into the airport, and you can't believe the airport. It's a madhouse. There are people sleeping all over the place. There are bags all over the floor. You've got to tiptoe your way through the airport. It was unbelievable. Naturally, we couldn't get our bags. It was incredible.

So there was no taxis. There was no cabs. There was nothin'. No limousines. But we had Johnny Bucyk, our captain. Everybody knows Johnny Bucyk—500 goals scored, left winger, one of the best of all time.

He was one of those guys that was like a sergeant in the army when you're overseas. What he did was he was a finagler. So he goes to the limo guy and he says, "You got any limos?"

"No limos."

So he says to the guy, "How much does it cost for a limo into the Drake Hotel?"

The guy says, "A hundred bucks."

Johnny says, "How does three hundred sound to you? Get ready. We'll be ready."

So sure enough, here come the limos. There's about five of them. They were lined up. Money talks.

We were in one of them and a little old lady was trying to get in, and I swear one of the guys closed the door on her. He almost closed it on her hand. I felt bad. It was like Bangladesh. You couldn't believe it.

So finally we get to the hotel and when we get to the hotel, all the homeless people and the street people are sleeping in the lobby to keep warm. It was something to behold.

So now we go down for the game the next day and our equipment is in San Francisco!

But the one thing that had come through was our underwear, believe it or not. The guys are sitting there in the dressing room in their underwear, playing cards.

So I go up to watch Chicago come out and I tell you, there was nothing like it. The Chicago Stadium and that organ, it gave me chills.

Keith Magnuson, God love him, when he'd come out, he had the long blond hair and they'd play "Here Come the Hawks" and Keith would go flyin' around with his hair flowin' out behind him. I tell you, I loved it.

Anyhow, they were upstairs warming up and we were playing cards. After about half an hour, they'd had their warmup and our equipment came.

We went out and, naturally, smoked 'em.

AL'S NOTE: *Keith Magnuson was killed December 15, 2003, in a car accident just north of Toronto.*

* * *

I'm often asked which building I always thought was the best building for hockey and atmosphere. Well, the Boston Garden, for sure, was one of them, but the Chicago Stadium was sorta special.

They had everything goin' for them then. I loved the timer in Chicago Stadium. If you were up by one goal and there was ten seconds left and you were in your end and there were three faceoffs, somehow you'd look up and there would be still ten seconds left.

That timer there was a beauty. One time, it even gained a couple of seconds!

But I'll tell you one thing. If *they* were up by one and there was ten seconds left and the faceoff was in *their* end, as soon as the puck dropped, the game was over!

I remember the very first time they used the foghorn, Bill Wirtz's foghorn. A lot of people don't know it, but it was from his yacht, the *Black Hawk*. The very first time it was used, the Boston Bruins were in there.

We were on the bench and the Hawks were kinda lookin' down at us 'cause they knew what was comin' and we didn't. Sure enough, they scored a goal and they let loose with that foghorn.

Well, I'll tell you, you should have seen our guys jump.

The Chicago guys had the funniest time laughin' at us. It was one of the loudest of all. I almost fell to my knees.

* * *

This is a story, and it's a true story of Bobby Orr, the year before I got there when Oakland was in the league. And the story goes like this.

Bobby Orr was killin' a penalty and somehow or other, he lost his glove at centre ice. Now, you remember how Bobby used to go behind the net and they'd chase him and he'd come out in front of the net? So nobody ever really went at him—and I've got another story about that one.

But he's still killing the penalty with one glove. He's got the puck at centre ice and he skates backwards, and as he skates backwards, he leans down and puts his glove on. He skates behind his net, killin' the penalty.

All of a sudden he roars up the right side, ninety miles an hour, as they say, goes around the defenceman, shoots it on the goaltender.

The goaltender goes to catch it, but it goes up in the air out of his glove. Bobby, as he goes behind the net, takes it and smacks it into the far corner.

Guys that were there said it was the first time that guys on both benches got up and banged their sticks on the boards. It's hard to believe, but I was telling the story about it one time with a bunch of guys and one guy, Gary "Suitcase" Smith, said, "Grapes, that's a true story."

I said, "How do you know, Gary?"

And he says, "Because I was the goalie and you had to see it to believe it."

* * *

I'll give you one more story of Bobby killin' a penalty. As I said before, you did not want to run at him when he had the puck in his end because if you ran at him, he'd go and hide behind the net. And then if you went for him behind the net, he'd go out in front. He'd go round and round and he'd kill the penalty all by himself.

Well, one time I was coaching, very early in my career. I think it was about a week into the season, so I hadn't really seen any of his end-to-enders, as they say. So he's got the puck behind our net killing a penalty—in the second period, I'll never forget it.

He comes down very slowly down the right side. He doesn't want to go too far, but they're not going to run at him because they know that he'll go and hide behind the net.

So they're kind of playing it cozy—Atlanta. They let him get over the red line. They let him get over the blue line, their blue line.

Now he goes into the corner and for some reason, I've never seen it before, every guy on the team went after him—in the corner.

Well, he turned on the power and they all fell down. This is a true story, I got it on tape.

And as he went to go behind the net, the goalie came out to stop him from going behind the net, to take the puck off him. He missed him and fell down. Bobby come around the front and backhanded it into the net. There was an absolute silence. It was the first time, and the only time, I ever heard a five-second silence after a goal because people couldn't believe what they saw. And all of a sudden, the people went nuts.

And you know what Bobby did? He looked back and saw what he had done.

He put his head down, as he used to do, put his stick across his knees and coasted out. He felt bad. He put head down because he felt bad that he had embarrassed everybody. I tell this story and I'm getting misty.

* * *

When I was lookin' through the pictures that are goin' into this book, I started thinkin' about the Bruins' power play.

I remember my first practice as coach of the Bruins. Towards the end, I called the team together at centre ice.

I said, "Okay, I'll take the rest of the team at this end. John Bucyk, you take the power-play guys and work on it at the other end."

The players looked at me as if I was kiddin'. A player is going to run the power play?

I said, "What? I'm gonna tell Johnny Bucyk and Phil Esposito and Bobby Orr how to run a power play?"

* * *

There is a picture in the book of Phil and Bobby saluting the fans during the Last Hurrah at the Boston Garden.

Between them, they scored 2,697 points. What a power play! Bobby blasting from the point. Wayne Cashman in front, screening the goalie. And if the goalie saved it, Phil zinging home the rebound.

If there wasn't an opening for Bobby to blast it, he would do the spinnerama, and if there still wasn't an opening for Bobby to blast it, then he would slip it over to 500-goal scorer John Bucyk, who would roof it. It was somethin' to see.

The bumper sticker around Boston read, "Jesus saves but Esposito scores on the rebound."

Phil still holds the record for shots on goal in a season. He had over 500.

See Bobby's big knees. His shin pads were filled with cotton batting to protect his knees. He would add layer after layer. Guys with bad knees should try it.

There was a standing ovation for two of the best. Don't you think the picture is sort of sad? I do.

* * *

Remember Al Arbour? He coached the New York Islanders to four Stanley Cups in a row. They used to call him "Radar" because I think he was the last guy to play with glasses. That's why they called him Radar, because he couldn't find his way around without glasses.

Al tells about the time we were in Rochester and he was having a tough time getting babysitters. He finally gets this babysitter, but she's a little worried because she has heard about hockey players being a wild group. It was a young babysitter, the first time she'd ever been a babysitter, and Al told her, "Oh yes, I'm very responsible. I'll be home early after the game."

So he only had a couple of beers after the game and he come

home early. His wife, Claire, was going to pay off the babysitter and Al was going to take the dog out. He's at the top of the stairs to the cellar and reaches down to put the leash on the dog, but when he clips the leash to the collar, the dog gets excited and pulls away. Al takes a header down the cellar stairs and opens up a big cut on his forehead.

There was blood all pouring down over his face and the little babysitter opened the door and came out and there's Al standing there with blood all over his face.

The last he ever saw of his new babysitter, she was screaming as she went running down the road.

* * *

People always ask me who's the toughest guy I ever played with or played against. When you spend your career in the minors, there are a lot of them. Connie "Mad Dog" Madigan. Sandy "Stone Face" Hucul and Bill "The Destroyer" Shvetz. I'll talk about those guys later.

But I think the nastiest guy I ever saw was Larry "The Rock" Zeidel. He was from Montreal and I played with him in my second year in Hershey. I don't know how he got to our club, but he got to our club and he was my partner, and I knew there was going to be problems. He said that when we set up behind the net, when he's in one corner and I'm in the other and he's got the puck, that we should holler plays like football. We should holler "X" or "Y" or "Z."

I'm thinking, "Oh boy, this guy is really something."

I remember when we were on the road and we got new gloves and Obie O'Brien, our captain, went to see a doctor in Cleveland, and while Obie was in there, all of a sudden, the bottles started to bounce all around in the doctor's office. Larry was out in the waiting room and he was punchin' the walls. He said, "Hey, we gotta break these gloves in."

* * *

Larry was always upset that I was going to beat him in the penalty parade. It was always a big thing for him to be first in penalties. I don't think I ever did beat him. I think he beat me all the time.

This one time in Cleveland, I got into the penalty box with a player called Ian Cushenan. Now it's hard to believe it in this day, but we all used to sit in the same penalty box! There would always be a policeman in there, that's for sure.

So Ian and I got yapping away at one another and we started to fight, and it was really something. We were back and forth. There was no glass behind the net in those days. It was wire mesh. We wouldn't stop.

Finally, they had to go and call in more police. We were wrecking the place and one of those policemen down there put a billy club on my forehead. He just tapped me. And I tell you, I never felt a clunk like that.

He said, "You ready to settle down, son?"

I said, "Yes sir."

So I look up and there's Larry and he's grabbing the penalty box door. He tears it off and he throws it out on the ice! He gets a game misconduct, the whole deal. The reason he did it was because he thought I'd go ahead of him in penalty minutes!

The night before, he woke me up as I was sleeping. He had bought a paper. He never slept. He always went out late. He never drank or partied, but he just couldn't sleep and when that happened, he'd go for a walk.

He said, "Look, you're beating me in the penalty parade." So he made sure I didn't beat him that night.

AL'S NOTE: *Ian Cushenan went on to play for four NHL teams—Chicago, Montreal, New York Rangers and Detroit. Larry Zeidel played in the NHL for Philadelphia. Don stayed in the AHL. He once said, "I needed every bit of toughness at my command. Toughness with the fist and toughness with the stick because my opponents were ruthless. They'd put their stick right through me if they were given a chance. So I had to be sure and hit first."*

* * *

Larry was really something—nasty like you wouldn't believe.

The very first night I saw him in action, he cut a player—Ray Hannigan, a tough Irish winger.

Hannigan was sitting beside me in the penalty box and I'm watching the blood come out of the side of his head. The cut was on his temple and the blood was just pumping with his heart.

His own players were trying to get him out of the penalty box and he was saying, "No way. I'm going to get that SOB!"

Can you imagine sitting there watching the blood? Larry didn't even get a penalty, which drove Hannigan nuts. They finally got Hannigan off because he started to get weak from the loss of blood. Those Hannigan boys were tough lads.

* * *

Speakin' of Cleveland, I was playin' there once and I got cut in the third period between the eyes. But I kept on playin'. There was only about five minutes to go, only a couple of shifts, so I kept on playin' until the game was all over.

The doctor came down and he had figured the game was all over because it was so late, and he had been drinkin'.

So I had to lay down. In the middle of the dressing room, as a lot of people know, there's a table where you put the oranges and towels and stuff like that, bottles and everythin'.

So that's where I laid down. You could hardly see. It was dark in the place and here's a guy stitching up my eye. I was looking up and he was sweating because he had been drinking. I could hardly see his face and he's gonna stitch up my eye.

The guys were taking a shower. The shower door was ten feet

away from where he was stitchin' up my eye. The fog was comin'
out and the steam was comin' out and I could hardly see him and
the guys are so blasé about me getting cut.

Here's a guy stitchin' my eye. He can hardly see. The fog's
comin' out and he's been drinkin' and the guys are shoutin', "Come
on, Grapes, hurry up. The bus is leavin'."

They were thirsty I guess. It's a wonder I'm still so pretty.

* * *

When I started out in the American Hockey League, when they
stitched you up, it wasn't like in *Slap Shot*. Nobody ever got
stitched on the bench. That was ridiculous.

But it was just behind the bench, so it was almost the same.

I remember my very first bad stitches. I was playing for Hershey
and I went down to block a shot. It cut my lip all the way up to my
nose.

I sat on the bench in the dressing room and the floor was wood.
And believe it or not, in those days, they didn't have those plastic
tips on the back of the skates. They were sharp, and they almost
went to a point. I remember the doctor standing between my legs
and stitching me up on my lip. They never froze you. Forget the
novocaine. What was that?

When it was finished, I was in such pain that I'd driven my skates
into the floor, because the floor was wood. The trainer had to pull
out my skates, if you can believe it. And we did it for $4500 a year.

* * *

Gretzky was in the hunt for his 50th goal in December 1981 and we
were going out to do the game, I think it was with Tim Spelliscy,
and we were going out to Edmonton do the game for *Hockey Night
in Canada*. Gretzky needed five goals. It was his 39th game and if
he could do it, it would be the record of records.

Before the game, I'm saying, "Well, you know it's a funny thing, I just have a feeling. . . ." and I was just kidding, of course. I had no feeling that he was gonna get 50 goals in 39 games, but I said, "Wouldn't it be something if we were out here on television and he gets his 50th goal in his 39th game? Wouldn't it be unbelievable?"

Sure enough, he gets the one. I'm gonna hurry it through. He gets two. He gets the hat trick. Now everybody's goin' nuts in the place. Really.

He gets four! He gets four goals, and I'm hurryin' this story through, but I remember that Philly had their goalie out and they were wearing those stupid coveralls, what did they call 'em?

They got Billy Barber back on the point and they've got the goalie out, and Gretzky could really fly when he wanted to fly. He breaks away and Billy Barber goes over and tries to jump and he falls down. Gretzky walks around him and scores his 50th goal. His 50th goal in 39 games!

I said, "He scores his 50th goal in 39 games, when nobody else in the league has even reached 30."

So I'm walkin' out after, and I'm walkin' out beside Billy Barber and he's cursin' and swearing and sayin' "That no good son of a gun" and everything.

I said, "What's the problem, Billy? I know you lost, and I know he scored 50, but what's that got to do with you?"

He said, "Thirty years from now, they'll be showin' that 50th goal and they'll show me fallin' down as he goes around me."

I said, "No Billy. No they won't."

And you know what? I just saw it again on *Hockey Night in Canada* and they said, "There's Billy Barber fallin' down."

You were right, Billy.

AL'S NOTE: *They called them Cooperalls because they were made by the Cooper sporting goods company. The Flyers started wearing them in 1981–82, and the Hartford Whalers followed suit, so to speak, in 1982–83. But they were universally reviled and were banned by the NHL at the end of that season.*

* * *

When people see me at the opening of "Coach's Corner," standing up on the bench, extending my arms, letting on I'm taking a bow, they think I'm showin' off to the crowd and acknowledging the cheers.

That's not true.

It was what coaches do when they think the referee is calling penalties and doing it for the crowd. That's what you do. Other coaches clap. I happened to get up and do that. It looked pretty good, I must admit.

Everybody thinks it was the too-many-men penalty that was called in the 1979 semifinal. That's not true either.

But it was the same period.

First, if you can believe it, Jean Ratelle, the Lady Byng winner, actually had a penalty for high-sticking Bob Gainey. What happened was, Bob Gainey ran at him with an elbow and he just put up his stick to protect himself and he got Gainey with the stick. So Ratelle got it for high-sticking.

The one where I'm bowing came right after that. We were up 3–1 and the referee, who was Bob Myers, gave Dick Redmond, one of our defencemen, a penalty for cross-checking Jacques Lemaire — who he hardly touched, but he went down.

So it wasn't the too-many-men penalty. That came next. What I was doing was acknowledging that the crowd had called the penalty to Redmond.

It's a strange thing. Bob Myers, he was also the referee that put Toronto out in the series before that. He gave Tiger Williams a penalty in overtime and Larry Robinson scored on the power play.

Tiger Williams come out of the penalty box and tried to attack Myers. They had to almost tackle him to hold him back. Larry Robinson, on the other team, had to hold Tiger.

Funny, eh? Same referee put out Toronto the time before — and us.

* * *

Montreal, back in those days, had something goin' for 'em. After every goal, the whole team would jump on the ice and congratulate the guy who scored.

It was very intimidating to see the whole other team jumping around, and they did this perfectly.

So before the series, a guy from Canada had seen them play and told me, "Look, you've got to do something about this."

So in the team meeting before the first game, I said, "This is what I want. If Montreal jumps on the ice after the first goal, everybody on our team jump on too. Everybody!"

They looked at me as if I was nuts.

I said, "Everybody jump on and get out there and congratulate Cheevers."

So sure enough, they get the first goal. They all jump on. We jump on. There's forty guys milling and jumpin' around, pushing one another.

So the referee, Dave Newell, come to me and says, "You can't do this. You can't send somebody on the ice."

I says, "Whaddya mean I can't send somebody? They send their guys on the ice."

He says, "Yeah, but you can't be doin' this. You're not supposed to send your guys on the ice for your goalie."

I said, "Every time they go out on the ice after a goal, our team is goin' out too."

So they had a meeting and from that minute on, they stopped the whole team from comin' out on the ice to congratulate the guy who got the goal.

So that's one rule I put in. I'm sort of sorry, in a way. I'd like to see the teams all come on after a goal.

* * *

One night, when I was with Rochester—we were playin' Pittsburgh—I got in a fight with this Dennis Hextall. He pushed Darryl Sly, and I got in a fight with him and we were goin' pretty good, then the linesman tied me up.

I'll never forget the linesmen's names. The guy that had me tied up was Lou Chantral. The guy that was supposed to have Dennis Hextall tied up was Ed House.

I was all tied up like you couldn't believe and Dennis didn't have his right hand tied up. I looked over and Dennis, he actually smiled.

He hit me for a beauty. Stitches wouldn't stop forever.

So I'm getting stitched up—and when you get stitched up they always say, "Just one more. Just one more." They said that so you'll get ready for the one more and then they say, "Well, maybe we'd better add another one." So I was gettin' one more, one more, seventeen times. It was a beauty. Think about it. Seventeen stitches on your eye. It looked like I had three eyes.

So Rose is waitin' outside where the wives always wait, all the players are walkin' by and Jimmy Pappin says, "Oh Rose, he's got a beauty this time."

So I did finally get out and it was still seepin' blood a little. And Rose come up. I thought she was going to be kind of, you know, sorry for me and that.

She looks at me and she says, "I never knew a fist could do that much damage."

* * *

We always used to go to the Downtowner in Rochester. It was a lovely restaurant owned a guy by the name of Merle Sweet. He used to give us sandwiches. We'd buy the beer and everythin', but he'd put sandwiches out because we hadn't eaten since meal time.

So we're havin' a good time drinkin' the beer and eatin' the sandwiches, but the sandwiches are all done and my eye was still seeping blood out, and I was holding ice on it with these serviettes because it was startin' to swell.

Well, startin' to swell? It had swelled. I was tryin' to get it down.

So the blood kept soaking the serviettes. I kept using them and throwing them in those little wicker baskets that they put sandwiches in 'cause the sandwiches were all gone, like I said.

So here's this basket full of bloody serviettes and a young waitress come along and she went to pick it up and she screamed.

Anyhow, I had a black eye and the whites of my eyes were red for eight months after that. He got me good, I have to admit.

*　*　*

Dennis Hextall was a good tough player, a good fightin' player, you'd better believe it. One time when I was coachin' the Bruins, we were playing in Detroit in the Olympia and Gary Doak turned back. He was behind the net and he was goin' along the boards, and he turned back and Hextall nailed him and crushed his cheekbone. It was broken and there was blood all over.

I told the players after, "Keep your mouth shut. Remember, forewarned is forearmed. When we get in the dressing room after and you're asked about it, keep your mouth shut and say, 'It's part of the game.' That's what I'm gonna say. But let's not forget."

That was all I said, "Let's not forget."

Well, from then on, every time we played Hextall, one or the other would always get him. Every game, he knew, when he was going to face the Boston Bruins, he was going to be in a fight with one of the Bruins—and believe me, we had the toughest of them all.

We even followed him around to different teams. Then, after the game, even though he had played good, I'd say, "You know, it's sad to see Dennis Hextall the way he's playing. How sad to see a good player playin' like that."

Actually, he had played pretty good, but I was gettin' him.

So then he goes to Washington, and one of my lovely pit bulls, an English bull terrier, Stan Jonathan, got him and did he do a number on him! When the fight was over, Stan got a two-minute minor, a five-minute major, a ten-minute misconduct and a game misconduct. And guess what Hextall got? Nothing! So you know how the fight went.

John McCauley, God love him, was refereeing and I said, "Hey McCauley, just because you win the fight, do you have to get all those penalties?"

He come over and he says, "That's somethin' *you* never had to worry about, eh, Cherry?"

The players loved it.

AL'S NOTE: *Dennis Hextall played no fewer than 681 games over thirteen seasons in the NHL with New York Rangers, Los Angeles, California, Minnesota, Detroit and Washington. His father, Bryan, had also played eleven seasons with the New York Rangers from 1936–1948, and his brother Bryan was an established NHLer as well, playing with five teams over eight seasons.*

As Don says, Dennis was "a good tough player." With his career penalty-minute total of 1,443, he was in no danger of getting his name on the Lady Byng Trophy.

* * *

A lot of people ask, "What's the toughest team you've ever seen?" Well I just have to tell you a few stories on that.

I have to start with Dave "The Hammer" Shultz. If you read his book—and if you don't know, he was with the Broad Street Bullies, which was a pretty tough team—and he put in his book that he could not sleep the night before he went into the Boston Garden because he knew he had to fight at least five guys if he acted up.

He put in his book, "We had five tough guys, but they had five tough guys who were psycho," and he said he could not sleep.

The funny thing is, Paul Holmgren told a friend of mine—I think it was Scott Mellanby—that he could not sleep the night before he went in the Boston Garden.

He said to Scott, "If I didn't get John Wensink, in the next shift I'd get Stan Jonathan and then I'd get Al Secord and then sometimes Wayne Cashman."

He said, "They had four wingers and I knew it was going to be a war."

We used to work it that way. We'd never ever beat a team bad. We'd just beat them 4–1. You know, never run up a score, never embarrass anybody.

With Minnesota, they'd come in and we'd never beat 'em bad, like I said. Just 5–2, 5–1, somewhere in there, and they'd never really put up a fight and that's the way we wanted it.

This is a true story. Here's what Harry Sinden did. Harry actually went on—get this—actually went on Minnesota TV and said, "It's a shame that your players don't play harder against the Bruins in this building to put on a show for our fans."

I just happened to be watching it. I was flicking around for some reason in between periods and I put it on for the players to see. If you can imagine—the general manager of a team telling the other team to play harder against his team!

We had wars after that. Before that, we had it easy and after that, we never had an easy game with Minny.

AL'S NOTE: *Harry Sinden was the general manager of the Bruins at the time. There's no need for me to say much more about him here. Don will have plenty to say about him.*

The Broad Street Bullies were the Philadelphia Flyers of the 1970s. They got the name because the Flyers played in the Spectrum, which is on Broad Street, and they were bullies more than enforcers. They tended to fight in packs, especially if there were some perceived slight to their captain, Bobby

Clarke. They had some quality players, especially Clarke and goaltender Bernie Parent, but they also had a number of guys who tended to take a physical toll on the opposition. They included Shultz, Don Saleski, Andre "Moose" Dupont, Bob "Mad Dog" Kelly and the Watson brothers, Jim and Joe. The Broad Street Bullies won the Stanley Cup in 1974 and 1975.

* * *

In the Boston Garden, we used to try to keep the shots down as low as we could and I remember Emile Francis, he was with St. Louis at the time, he come in to scout us.

We were playing some team, and they didn't put up much of a show and we beat them, which was the way we liked it, and they only had thirteen shots.

Emile Francis went on TV and said, "That's a disgrace for a team to come in and have only thirteen shots on net and put on a show like that."

St. Louis, his team, came in next. That's why he was there scoutin'. And *they* only had eleven shots!

* * *

This one was told to me second-hand because I wasn't in Boston when Kevin Lowe started comin' in with the Oilers.

But he told a friend of mine one time, "I just hated playing in the Boston Garden, that little building, that little wee bit of ice and those great big monsters coming. That team had it down perfect. They'd flip it in and we used to call it 'leansies.' They'd flip it in and the puck would actually lean up against the wall. I had to go in first, and here's these monsters coming in."

He said, "I was on first-name basis with everybody in the first row. My face was jammed up against the glass every night."

* * *

A lot of people ask, "How did Blue ever get to be so famous?" They were going to make her the official dog in Boston instead of the Boston terrier.

What happened was, it was by accident. A reporter—his name was Tom Fitzgerald, God love him—he came in and he said, "Who's playin' in goal tonight?"

I happened to say, "Well, Cheevers always plays good against the New York Rangers and Blue says to play him."

It was a joke. So Cheevers shuts out New York Rangers.

Tom come in the next game and says, "Well, who does Blue say is goin' tonight?"

I just happened to say, "Not Gerry Cheevers. Gillie Gilbert is going tonight."

I forget which team it was, but Gillie got a shutout.

So it got to be a funny thing. I was just kiddin'.

So it caught on and it was a joke, but it really wasn't a joke because a lot of people don't know that I really, really did pattern the Bruins after my first Blue, and I'll tell you why.

We never, ever went lookin' for trouble as long as you let us have our way, and Blue never ever did pick on a smaller dog or go really looking for trouble, like throwin' the first punch.

But sometimes, she used to put herself in the way so that you would have to do somethin', and that's the way I had the Bruins. I'd put them so that the guy would have to react—like a little push afterwards, or a stare or somethin' like that, but never take the first punch.

That's a true story with Blue, and let me tell you, she was in a few fights but she never started one though.

* * *

Let me tell ya a little story about attitude that she taught me and my son Tim about life. We were on Wolfe Island and a lady that lived next door to us had a visitor who had two enormous Great Danes. One was a smoke. It was a grey dog, a great big dog, about 150 pounds, and it had orange eyes, if you can believe it. The other was a Harlington, and a Harlington is a black and white dog.

They were up from New York and the girl's name was Debbie. Why she had these two monsters, I don't know. It actually ended up that they had to be put down. About a year later, they cut her for about ninety-two stitches.

Anyhow, they're nuts. These dogs are cuckoo. They had already attacked a couple of people on the island, and for some reason, I was going over there. I don't know why, but I forgot they were there. I had a bushel basket in my hand and they started after me. I got in a corner and kind of held them off with this bushel basket for about ten seconds.

It looked like they were going to kill me, but Debbie got there fast and took the dogs and let me get back to my place.

The next morning I wake up early, and I'm kind of half-asleep and I open the door to let Blue out. Well, those two dogs weighed about 125 to 150 pounds apiece and here are the two of them at the bottom of the stairs. Blue weighed about forty-five pounds.

Well, I said, "This is it. These two dogs are going to tear her to shreds."

I couldn't stop her because she had seen them as well.

She goes strutting down there with her tail stiff as a board like you wouldn't believe, kind of stiff-legged, like she's saying, "Come on, you stiffs. What are you doin' over here? What are you doin' over on *my* land?"

She goes over and she's brushing up against them, daring them to fight! They don't know. What the hell is this thing comin'? And she's pushing up like she's saying, "Get out of here," with a chip on her shoulder.

And they're terrified of her. Believe it or not, these two monsters that have already ripped dogs to shreds there and cut a guy up and later cut Debbie for ninety-two stitches were terrified of her.

She's brushing up against them and they slowly backed up, then ran home.

I says, "There you are, Tim. I was looking for a hammer to go down and help her when those dogs attacked. Attitude is everything. If she hadda ran, she was dead. But she went up and pushed up against them and they were terrified of her."

And a little epilogue, or whatever you call it, is that Debbie come up to see Rose and she was sitting in the living room. These dogs come up and were looking in the screen door.

Blue saw them and ran at the door and growled and they ran away home.

I swear she looked at me as if to say, "Yeah, Dad. Piece of cake!"

* * *

Another time with Blue, I saw her attitude. Are ya kinda gettin' the idea that I loved her? I was walking along the same island, Wolfe Island. Same next door. This year, they had four golden retrievers.

Now, I know golden retrievers aren't the most ferocious dogs in the world, but these dogs are about eighty pounds and they put on a pretty good show.

I'm taking Blue for a walk and as we walk past the place down the road, out come these four golden retrievers comin' ninety miles an hour. They're roarin'.

Blue turns. It wasn't like she was shocked or she was goin' at 'em. She just turned and walked straight at them, all nonchalant, smellin' the ground.

Well, again, these dogs are thinkin', "What the hell? Here we are barkin' and chargin' and this here little dog comes walking straight at us. What's goin' on?"

So she just went from one side to the other. And each time, she's backing them up. Back and back. Nudge, nudge, nudge. She's got her eye on them, but she's just smellin' as she's going along. Three of them disappeared and one of them kept backin' up. She wouldn't let this one alone. She was ticked that they ran at her.

So this one got down and crouched in front of their cottage and Blue just kept walkin' towards it and walked in front of the dog, and the lady—the owner—come out.

Well, as soon as the other dog saw her, he got a little brave and attacked Blue.

Well, that's just what Blue wanted. She wouldn't attack—the dog attacked Blue.

You shoulda seen it. It was beautiful, I tell ya.

She knocked it down and held it down. She wouldn't hurt it— golden retrievers, she didn't think much of them. She held it down and the lady was screaming.

I said, "Blue, let it up." She just let it up and just kept on walkin' as if it was nothin'.

We just walked home and as soon as we got around the corner, I picked her up and I said, "You're the greatest thing that ever walked on *any* number of feet."

* * *

Eddie Shore, "The Edmonton Express" because he had played in Edmonton even though he was from Saskatchewan, was a mean, nasty guy who could take pain and he loved to dish it out. I think the more you hurt him, the better he liked it. And I *know* he liked to hurt the other guy.

He used to come out on the ice with a cape, if you can believe it. He thought he was Superman. He was a Saskatchewan boy and he started out as a bronco buster. He didn't start skatin' until it was kinda late, but once he took to it, look out!

He had more injuries, and was he tough! He played with stitches in his leg and when they broke open, he just kept on playin'. There was blood all over the place. One game, he had a broken jaw and a broken nose, lost some of his teeth and kept on playin'.

One practice, he almost lost his ear and the doctor wanted to cut it off. Eddie said, "There's no way you're cuttin' it off," and he went and found a doctor who would work on it, and believe it or not, he didn't take any painkillers or needles or anything.

He even put the needle where he wanted it and told the guy how to sew him up right. He knew everything. He really did. Even how to be a surgeon. He had everything down pat.

AL'S NOTE: *Eddie Shore is one of the greatest figures in hockey history. He was born in Fort Qu'Appelle, Saskatchewan, in 1902, and earned the nickname "The Edmonton Express" when he became a first-team all-star playing defence for the Edmonton Eskimos in the 1925–26 season. He went on to become the first four-time winner of the Hart Trophy as the NHL's most valuable player.*

He was on the first Boston Bruins team to win the Stanley Cup, and towards the end of a storied career, negotiated a deal that allowed him to play in the NHL while owning, managing and playing for the Springfield Indians of the American Hockey League.

He was inducted into the Hall of Fame in 1947 and died in 1985.

* * *

Shore thought he was a chiropractor, doctor, rocket scientist, everything. If you ever thought you had a headache or a cold or anythin', he always thought it came from your neck, if you can believe it.

He did it to me once. He had monstrous hands for a little guy, and he'd grab your neck. He'd twist your neck and try to crack your neck. He'd holler, "Relax! Relax!"

How can you relax when he's tryin' to break your neck?

So we're all in the dressing room waitin' to go out one time, and some guy makes the mistake of saying he didn't feel well, so Eddie goes and grabs the guy's head and starts twistin' it this way, twistin' it that way, twistin' it this way.

There was a guy named Dennis Olsen who really had a dry sense of humour and we're all quiet, sittin' there, and out of the blue sky, Dennis looks at Eddie and he says, "Eddie, can I ask you a question?"

Eddie just glares at him and says, "Yes."

And Dennis says, "Did one of those ever come off in your hands?"

Eddie was not amused.

* * *

One time, Eddie missed a train to Montreal, took a taxi and drove a total of twenty-two hours. The cab driver drove for a long time but was scared to drive any further, so Eddie took it over, got the cab into a ditch, and got it out again. He made it after twenty-two hours. He made it to Montreal just in time for the game.

He scored the winning goal. They won 1–0 and he got fined for missing the train. They were tough in those days.

He broke his nose thirteen times. He had over a thousand stitches. Most of his teeth were gone. Like I said, he lost most of his ear.

He almost killed Ace Bailey hitting him from behind. You get the idea! He was a little tough as a player.

He was an even tougher owner and coach. Everybody said he was eccentric. I said he was nuts.

AL'S NOTE: *Shore was playing for the Boston Bruins on December 12, 1933, in a game against the Toronto Maple Leafs when he hit Ace Bailey from behind.*

There were no helmets in that era, and Bailey's head hit the ice so hard that he was knocked unconscious. The injury appeared to be so serious that a priest was summoned from the crowd to administer last rites.

Bailey survived, but never played again.

Two months later, a benefit game was played in Maple Leaf Gardens to raise money for Bailey. This was the first NHL All-Star Game, but it did not become an annual event until 1947.

Shore, by the way, did not escape NHL justice. He was suspended for six-teen games.

* * *

One guy who wasn't really afraid of Eddie Shore was Marcel Paille.

Marcel Paille was a goalie with the New York Rangers and was sent down to Springfield for a while for punishment, so he wasn't really afraid of Eddie like the rest of us.

We were down 3–0 one game and Marcel was in the nets. After the period ended, Eddie come in and blamed me for a goal and Marcel said, "No, Eddee. Dat was my fault."

So then Eddie went to Bill Sweeney and he said, "That second goal was your fault," and Marcel said, "No, Eddee. Dat was my fault."

Then Shore went to Dennis Olsen and he said, "That third goal was your fault," and Marcel said, "No, Eddee. Dat was my fault."

So Eddie glared at him and said, "So, then all three were your fault?"

And Marcel looked back at him and said, "Yeah, a 'at trick."

* * *

Some of the players told me that before I got there, he was even worse.

I couldn't believe it. He was so cheap, when I played there, we'd have a half-hour intermission between periods because they'd be sellin' booze—and everything to mix with the hard stuff.

Everywhere else, intermission would be about fifteen minutes.

Eddie owned the building and the concessions, so he'd put the players to work so he didn't have to pay a staff.

The day before the game, he'd give the players a big sack of peanuts and some paper bags.

The players would have to fill the bags but they had to do it properly. Eddie would say, "Remember now, twenty-five peanuts per bag."

* * *

Whenever I'm with Brian Kilrea, I always look at his watch. If it says one o'clock, it will be a quarter to one. I know why he does it. It's because when Eddie Shore would say, "Be on the ice at eleven," you had to be on the ice at quarter to. You'd better not be late. Even if you were on the ice at five to, you were late. Fifteen minutes ahead—we called it Eddie Shore time.

When you're late, it's funny how the guys react. You'd think they'd help their partner. Nope. The first thing they'd do when they knew a guy is late, they cut his skate laces. Then they cut his shoulder pads. And then some guys were even mean enough to cut his stick halfway through.

And then the funniest one of all is when you finally come on the ice, they all bang their sticks on the ice. Bang, bang, bang, bang. Just to make sure the coach knows you're late.

* * *

We were playing for Rochester back in the sixties, and there was a sign up: "Everybody be on the ice at ten o'clock."

Well, Al Arbour was late. It was five to. He didn't have time to change and make the practice on time. So what he had to do, he ran out in his shoes, dressed, and he said to the coach, Joe Crozier, "Hey, I'm on the ice."

So the next time the sign goes up: "Everybody on the ice with their equipment."

So about a month later, Al was late and he grabs his equipment and he runs out and he's standing on the ice in his civvies and he says, "Hey, it says be on the ice with your equipment."

Crozier couldn't do anything.

So then the sign goes up: "Be on the ice with your equipment on."

They got him there.

* * *

I'm going to talk about a strike that I was involved in. The Rochester Americans, who I played for, were involved in a roundabout way. It was back in 1966–67 and it all started in Springfield.

It started with three players — Dale Rolfe, Dave Amadio and Bill White. They wanted a raise, and I remember Brian Kilrea, when we were sitting having a few pops, telling me this story.

They wanted a raise and they were terrific defencemen. They deserved it. Dale Rolfe went to the New York Rangers. Bill White went to the Chicago Blackhawks and Dave Amadio was always a good player.

One thing I remember about Dale Rolfe was the number that Dave "The Hammer" Shultz did on him when he was in New York. I never forgave Shultz for that. Dale Rolfe couldn't fight. He was a big guy — six foot five — but he couldn't fight and Shultz just carved him up.

Anyhow, I'm gettin' off the subject. Back in the minors, they wanted a $500 raise. Shore suspended them, but eventually he had to give in and he finally gave them the money.

It was the strangest thing. When they came back, they just happened to lose their very first game and Eddie — he used to do this all the time — suspended them for "indifferent play."

Then he fined them as well, and it just happened — what a coincidence and a surprise — the amount just happened to be the $500 that he had given them.

That's the kind of stuff they could do before there was a union.

* * *

After this, they said they were going to go on strike, and the guys get together and the leader is Brian Kilrea. Eddie loved Brian.

Brian wasn't even the captain, but they knew that Eddie Shore liked him and that he had the guts to stand up to Eddie. Believe me, he would. He was one of those guys who would risk his own job to stand up for somebody else.

So Brian being the guy he is, he went in and tried to get to Shore, but he didn't get to him. So he left the message that he wanted to talk to him, and that if he didn't, there was going to be trouble.

So Eddie Shore suspended him. The other guys didn't get suspended. They were okay. Brian got suspended.

But the players were going to stick together, so they all were on strike. "Well then," said Shore, "that's fine. That's it. If you're all on strike, you're all suspended."

So they were all suspended. He was like Darth Vader. He was unbelievable.

Anyway, there were demands from the players. They wanted hospitalization when they were hurt, and medical coverage. You had to play for Shore when you were hurt. If you didn't play, he'd suspend you. It really was incredible.

Anyway, he finally gave in and said, "Okay, you all can come back—except Kilrea."

There's poor Brian. He's getting the blame.

So they all said, "No. If Brian doesn't come back, then we're all not comin' back."

So he says, "Then you're all suspended."

You must remember how bad it was in Springfield, and I'll tell you how bad it was. When you were in the NHL and you acted up—like Gump Worsley one time was sent down, Larry Cahan same thing—if you acted up and they didn't like you, they'd say, "We're going to send you to Shore in Springfield."

It was like Devil's Island: "You'll get sent to Shore." These guys really did have it tough.

So he'd suspended them all when they stood up for Brian and he had the doctor—the team doctor—phone every one of them up and say, "If you don't come back, you're going to be suspended for life."

There were some young guys there, so they went and told Brian that they were worried that they might be suspended for life and Brian says, "Oh, you got that phone call? I got a call from Clarence Campbell, the president of the National Hockey League, that I'm going to be suspended for life. How do you like that one?"

* * *

So it finally come up that they should get Alan Eagleson.

Eagleson was Bobby Orr's agent, and they were negotiating back and forth. Eagle got right on Shore. They went back and forth, fighting and everything like that. Eagle really told him.

It came down that they were going to stay on strike.

This is where I come in, 'cause I played for the Rochester Americans at the time and we were a first-place club. We were dynamite. I think we won the Calder Cup that year. In fact, I know we did.

We were supposed to play them on a Saturday night. This was their showdown game. They were going on strike and they weren't playin'.

We were told they weren't playing, and it was funny. Our team, Rochester, they were stayin' in the same Charles Hotel in Springfield as Bobby and Eagle.

We were there for the game and I was comin' down on the elevator and Alan Eagleson and Bobby Orr — they didn't know me from Adam — they were going over to the rink.

So we thought for sure they weren't going to settle, that there wouldn't be a game. We weren't prepared. We were all having a good time. We didn't have anything to eat. We never had our nap. So we figured we'd go out and work up a little sweat because we had to go out, then we'd be off.

So we're out there skatin' around in the warmup, figurin' nothing's wrong, then all of a sudden, the Springfield Indians come flying out. It was unbelievable. They were flyin'. They had been told that Shore was goin' to Florida and that he was leavin' the team to his kid to run it. They were like men let out of prison.

I think they hammered us about 7–1. We hardly ever touched the puck.

And that's how the union got started.

* * *

Alan Eagleson saw that they were afraid of unions when he started that strike and that's when they started the Players' Association in the NHL.

They saw they could do something. This was the thing they needed to get it going. And eventually, Eagleson ran the union for the NHL players.

Brian was the guy who stood up and got it goin', and I'll tell you a funny thing that happened. He came to Rochester near the end of his career. He had a bad back. He couldn't hardly skate. He couldn't hardly sit down. And he went to the Players' Association. He had to go and get his back fixed with a few chiropractors and things like that and he went to the Players' Association and they didn't even answer him. He was a nobody. And here was Brian, the guy that started it.

To this day, he often says, "You know, I look at what's happening in hockey today with the union and stuff and I wonder if I did the right thing."

AL'S NOTE: *Alan Eagleson was, of course, a lawyer. He became the first executive director of the National Hockey League Players' Association but in 1994 was charged by a Massachusetts grand jury with racketeering and defrauding the NHLPA.*

In a plea-bargaining deal, he was sentenced to eighteen months in jail, but served only six—in a minimum-security facility close to his home in Toronto.

* * *

Brian Kilrea did not have an easy time when he quit hockey. He started a restaurant and it was doing well and he didn't have a real nice jacket, so I gave him one of my blazers from the Rochester Americans. He looked good. He was host—sittin' people down and stuff like that. All of a sudden, a guy asked him, "Would you like to coach the junior club?"

"Well," Brian says, "I'd kinda like to coach. I don't know whether I'd like junior or not."

Didn't know whether he'd like it or not!

He got behind the bench and he was an absolute master. The players absolutely loved him. Talk to Dougie Wilson. Talk to all the ex-players who played for him. They loved him, but he's tough on them. Don't think he isn't tough.

One star come in and he said, "I don't like my billet and I want to move. I'm sick of it. I want to move now."

So Brian says, "You come back in the afternoon."

So the kid comes back in the afternoon and Brian says, "You've been traded to Owen Sound."

The kid says, "Well, wait a minute. I didn't want to go to another team."

Brian says, "You wanted to move. You're out. Move."

AL'S NOTE: *Doug Wilson was a Norris Trophy winner as an NHL defence-man, and is, at this writing, the general manager of the San Jose Sharks. At any writing, he'd be one of the most respected people in hockey. In the 2002–03 season, Brian Kilrea won his 1,000th game as a coach in junior hockey. A few months later he was inducted into the Hockey Hall of Fame in the Builder category.*

* * *

Brian never has curfew for these kids, but they don't dare stay out late because they know that Brian's tough.

I remember we had a prospects' game and we had Daniel Briere on our team. He was one of the prospects, but he wouldn't come off, so that meant the other kids didn't get a chance to shine. He was short-shiftin' the other guy. But Brian, he just levelled him. We were both behind the bench. I was handlin' the forwards and he had the defence and Brian turned to me and said, "Bench him. Bench him. Don't play the little SOB." He was tough.

There was another kid that we had who was a number-one draft choice. A lot of people don't know that players go to have a nervous pee a little while before they go out. All players do.

Here this guy does it while the team is on their way out. Brian just levelled the kid. "Who do you think you are? What's your hockey stick doing sitting there? You can't go out and be like the rest of us?"

He's tough, but he's the winningest junior coach of all time and before I leave off talking about Brian, I'll tell ya, he does one thing no other coach does. During the practice he stands at centre ice for the whole practice. They're scrimmaging. They're just missin' him by inches and he stands there!

Now you could say, "Well, he does it with the Ottawa 67's 'cause they know him." He does it at the prospects' game! How he stands there during the scrimmages and line rushes is beyond me, but he does it.

And I would have to say that next to Toe Blake, he is the best coach I ever saw.

* * *

One day I got a call from Brian and he said, "Don, I have a good oppor-tunity in this. I can go and be an assistant coach on Long Island."

I said, "Brian, don't take it."

He says, "Don, they're gonna pay me $80,000. That's the most money I've ever earned."

"Brian, don't take it. You're making a big mistake. You are a head coach. There are people that can be assistant coaches, but some people can never be one. No way should you go. Some people can never be an assistant. You cannot go and dig pucks out of the net. The players will come to you and they will turn to you."

"And the other guys will be mad at you, so don't take it. Stay where you are. You should be a head coach in the National Hockey League not an assistant."

Well, he didn't listen to me. He went as an assistant. That's exactly what happened. All the players loved him. They were always hanging around him.

In fact, he told me that one time, the players all got together on Christmas Eve and went and sang carols out in front of his house. When they were in airports, they were always hanging around him.

Sure enough, after one year, they let him go and he went back to junior.

There are people who can be assistants, and I'm not knocking them. You have to have assistants.

But there are guys like Brian, like myself, who can never be anything but a head coach.

* * *

Brian has more than a thousand wins in junior hockey and he's the toast of the game. There has never been a junior coach like him. But if he had gone to the National Hockey League as a head coach, he would have done just as well.

But you know what? He says he's happy. To this day, he's riding the buses. How he does it, I don't know. You get into the Soo and it's a ten-hour trip. North Bay, Sudbury. He just goes along.

I say, "Brian, how do you do it?"

He says, "Don, as long as I have my peanuts and Anne Murray on the radio, I can go on forever."

* * *

Another time, Brian and I were at the Rochester camp in Toronto. You must realize that by that time, him and I were confirmed minor-leaguers, as they say.

We never had a chance. No matter how good we played at training camp, we were destined for Rochester. We knew that many times.

I'll tell you a little story about Punch Imlach at that training camp. By then, he was the GM of the Leafs.

Somehow or other, and I have no idea how it happened, I got mixed up in the Toronto Maple Leafs scrimmage. I have no idea how that happened. It was a real accident. I'll go along further and tell you about Ronnie Ellis.

Ronnie Ellis at the time was a rookie, and he put in the paper, "Well, I don't know whether to go to college or whether to play for the Leafs."

And I'm thinkin', "I'd give my eye teeth just to have one shot at the Leafs, and here this guy is dithering whether he wants to go to college or play in the NHL."

I don't know whether he was using it for a ploy or what, but anyway, it kinda ticked me off. So we're practising and we're scrimmaging and Punch and King Clancy and them are up there watchin', and down comes Ellis. He could really skate and I really nailed him good.

It was one of those ones where you really nail the guy and he goes flat and you're steppin' over him. All of a sudden, I hear this screaming: "Get that fifty-cent hockey player off the ice with that million-dollar hockey player."

I'm the fifty-cent guy and they're yelling, "Get him off. Get him off."

There I am, standing there, looking down at Ellis, watching the general manager of the Toronto Maple Leafs run down the aisle from the top to throw me off the ice.

Well, I'm not kidding. I got thrown off the ice. As I went off, I smashed my stick and threw it out on the ice.

There might have been a lot of guys on that team who were better, but they weren't tougher.

That was just to give you an idea of how we were thought of.

* * *

That was the very first time I'd ever seen at any training camp where anybody brought in a guy to deal with conditioning. They brought in two guys from the Royal Military College in Kingston who were physical instructors.

Well, they were doin' things that we'd never done. They didn't tell us what they were goin' to do that summer. They had us doin' groin exercises, ridin' bikes, liftin' guys and pushin' guys. We had no idea we were going to do this, so guys were pulling their backs and hurting their arms.

In fact, one guy, a goaltender, he was so tired when we were ready to leave that he fell off the stage where we were doin' it and broke his arm.

When I got with a partner, I'd look the guy in his eye and say, "Look, we're gonna go along with everythin' they say, but we're just playin' at this, remember? We're just playin' at it. Don't go too hard on me and I won't go too hard on you."

So that's what I'd do with my partners, you know? But not Brian. He tried to do it right and he hurt his back, and his back was never, ever the same again.

* * *

You couldn't believe how we got treated at this camp. We first walked in and we walked by the Leafs' dressing room—a great big, bright, beautiful dressing room all painted white. New equipment. New underwear. It was unbelievable. Nice and spacious.

We get to ours, and I swear to you, it was by the boilers and the hot-water tanks and everything, and the roof was so low you had to duck.

It was always wet because the Leafs had Tulsa as a farm team, too, and when we'd leave, Tulsa would come in. The room was always wet and damp. Your equipment was always wet and damp and you had to go out in the cold.

Socks were always wet. Never new underwear. And here we'd walk by the Leafs and they'd have brand new underwear all the time, equipment nice and dry, and one team dressing in there.

If the day was really bad—this was in the fall—we'd practise at eight o'clock so the NHL guys could sleep in. But if it was a nice, sunny day, they'd practise at eight so they could golf after.

* * *

Larry Hillman was one of the nicest guys you'll ever meet, but sometimes, when guys go to the National Hockey League, they get carried away and forget where they came from.

This happened to all of us in Rochester.

We had our training camp in Peterborough with the Maple Leafs, and we couldn't go out and drink in a bar because Punch had spies all over Peterborough. So we all drank in the Royal Canadian Air Force club.

We'd go in, and the American leaguers would sit in the kitchen—which we didn't mind. It was a nice kitchen. We knew our place.

And the NHL guys would sit in the living room with all the leather chairs—which we understood. That's the way life is.

So we're sitting there, and Larry Hillman has gone up to the National Hockey League. Now, we never went into the living room. *Ever.* It's like your *Upstairs Downstairs*, that TV show they used to have.

They understood this. They were big-timers. They had their nice leather chairs and a beautiful room.

We're all right. We're havin' a good time. The beer is close and cold and the bar is in there, and Larry Hillman—our captain the year before!—comes in and gets a tray of pickled eggs.

He puts these eggs on a tray and walks right past us into the living room with this tray of eggs for the National Hockey Leaguers to eat. A whole big tray of them for them to eat!

He doesn't even look at us. He just walks right by!

So I get up, walk into the living room, pull out a chair and sit down in the middle of all these so-called big-timers. They might have been better hockey players, but they weren't tougher than me, or at least I thought that way. And I proceeded to rip Larry Hillman to shreds.

"Aw, Larry. Oh, you're with your friends now, eh? With the big-timers now? Forgot all your friends from last year, eh? Forgot when we worked with you and you were our captain?"

And I ripped him for him for ten minutes. I was callin' him names and callin' them big-timers and waitin' for somebody to say somethin'.

I said, "We won't forget this, Larry."

But I have to mention here that Larry was a real good guy. He just made one mistake. He got carried away with the NHL. I really like Larry.

At the time, though, I said, "Someday, you'll be back and we won't forget."

Sure enough, Larry was sent down. And you know what was in his stall waitin' for him?

A pickled egg.

* * *

Here's what Joe Crozier did one time at training camp. He coached us in Rochester, but he lived in Vancouver, and he come in and said, "Look, I've bought a brand new Dodge Charger here. They're a lot more expensive in Vancouver. I want you to drive it out to Vancouver."

I said, "What? Are you kiddin'? It's training camp."

He said, "No. You know you're going to make our club, and you're not going to make the Leafs, so I want you to drive it out."

I said, "That'll take three or four days."

He said, "Yep, but that's what you've gotta do."

So I figured, "What the heck? I'm gonna make the club anyhow."

So I said, "I'll only go if Brian Kilrea goes with me."

So poor Brian. He got sucked in too, It took us three or four days. We'd drive 'til night, then stop and have a few pops and go to bed. I remember one time we had Chinese food. We were havin' a ball.

One time we got stopped by a Mountie. He was lookin' to get us. Here's two guys in a big, brand new red Charger. He looked in the back and we had a case of beer, but fortunately for us, it hadn't been cracked open.

So we got there. Joe got his red Charger out there. We practised in Vancouver for two days. We were like outcasts, then we flew back.

That's what they thought of us. We were confirmed minor leaguers. We were nothin'.

* * *

A lot of people don't realize, like I said earlier, that some of the skates had no little clip on the end. One of the Toronto guys—Tim Daly, I think it was, I'm not sure—come up with the idea of that clip on the end of the skates, 'cause what would happen was they'd sharpen them right down, down, down until it almost came to a point.

Well, one time my very first year that I was supposed to make Boston, it was gettin' near the end of training camp, I hit a guy and I'll never forget his name. It was Eddie Panagabko.

His skate come up and went through my skate! Right through the bottom of my skate and into the bottom of my foot! Then he fell over and ripped the bottom of my foot.

I was taken in to Dr. Hofstedder. He sewed up the bottom of my foot with no novocaine. Now, tickle your toes and your feet sometime, and you can imagine what that was like.

It was the only time that I've ever been stitched that I sobbed. I was done for six weeks, and they left me—no doctor came to visit me. I was in a place called the Cocoa Inn. It was like a semi-hotel in Hershey. I got no penicillin, I got no nothing. I was out four to six weeks, and how I ever made it without getting an infection is beyond me, but I did. Thank the Lord.

* * *

I came back and my very first game was in Providence. The first period I got into a fight. I lost the fight 'cause I wasn't in shape, and the guy sitting beside me says, "I can't believe that you lost that fight."

The guy I fought was Jimmy Bartlett and he did a pretty good number on me. I thought, "This son of a gun sittin' next to me, why didn't he take him on?"

So after the game, I take a shower. I've got tape on my foot. You know how most people, you have a callus on the side of your foot? Well, that's where the cut was. Well, the trainer was mad. Scotty Alexander, the trainer, he was mad about something and he ripped it and it was wet. He ripped the tape off as hard as he could and he pulled that callus off, right down to the meat, and blood was flying everywhere.

Now, my foot has just been cut with stitches and there's blood everywhere. It was just unbelievable.

Frank Mathers, the coach, looked at him and said, "He doesn't play the next game, you're fired!"

I had to play the next game. I would have played the next game anyhow, but that's the way it was in the minors. Survival of the fittest.

* * *

When I was a little boy, every night after supper, my dad used to sit down and take one of the Horatio Alger books. There was 135 of them. The theme was always the same. A boy is striving to get ahead in life and something happens to him. Usually, he's pretty poor. He starts the job and the boss's son somehow gets him in trouble, but through honesty and courage, he goes to the end.

I'm sure you've heard someone say, "His life story was like something out of Horatio Alger."

Well, every night, Dad would read these books and he'd have a bag of bridge mixture. They were candy. And he'd read half a chapter. I can still see his glasses on the end of his nose.

If it come to a part where you had to be honest and you had to be courageous, he'd stop and look, and he'd give me a candy and we'd talk about it. It really did sink in, when you're young like that, every night, hearing about honesty and being courageous.

So in the book, the hero was always at odds with authority and his bosses, and his bosses were always after him. And I think after a while, it got to me.

Every job I had and every general manager I had, I seemed to be at odds with them. I think it did teach me to be courageous and honest, but I think it really did have something to do with my being against authority.

So in one way, it worked, and in another way it didn't. But I can still see my dad, when it came to something about being courageous or honest, he'd stop and we'd discuss it. Horatio Alger. Great books. There are 135 of them and they were written in the 1800s.

* * *

Sometimes I wonder about this honesty thing. Is it honest or stupid? Let me tell you a story; you decide.

I'm with the Barrie Flyers on our march to the Memorial Cup. Two guys get caught for drinking while we were in Quebec, and Hap Emms was dead against drinking. He suspended the two jerks.

Our captain had a meeting and said, "Okay, we'll all say we were all drinking and he can't suspend us all."

I said, "Gee, I don't ever drink; my Mom and Dad."

He said, "We have to stick together."

Hap came bursting into our room at the hotel that night, asked my roommate. He says no he hasn't been drinking, he turns to me and asks, "Cherry, have you been drinking?" He was enormous, he had a big sheepskin coat on, a big fedora, water dripping off. He'd come in from the rain. I was in my bare feet, brushing my hair (I still have the brush to remind me). I am terrified. I said, "Yes."

"Your ticket to go home will be in the morning. You're suspended."

I can't sleep, sit up all night. My Mom and Dad, that's all I can think of. I get on the elevator the next day and look at the captain. He wouldn't look me in the eye. I was the only one who said yes.

I'm sick, I don't ever drink. I'm suspended. What am I going to do? I'm not going home, for sure. This will kill my mom—she's also dead against drinking.

I get a call. The two jerks have asked for a meeting with Hap. I go along. I'll never forget the pleading for mercy. One guy, I kid you not, got down on one knee and cried. Hap turned to me, "You got anything to say?"

"Nope!"

"You want to go home suspended?"

"Nope." Screw it if my life is over before it began. I'm not going down begging.

His wife, Mabel, was in the next room. "What do you think, Mabel?"

"Oh, Hap, think of their parents. What if it was Paul?," their son.

So he turned to us and reamed us pretty good. "Get out of here. I'm so disappointed in you guys. This is your one and only chance. I'll be keeping my eye on you guys."

We went on to win the Memorial Cup. I often wonder what I would have done if he had followed through and suspended me, how my life would have been different. My Dad always told me to keep a promise, but as I look back now, I should have been smarter, I should have known those guys would bail.

Thank you Lord for keeping me in the club, but most of all, thank you for not having me go back to my Mom and Dad and tell them I'd been suspended for drinking.

* * *

Somehow or other, in my meanderings though life in the minor leagues, I ended up in the Montreal Canadiens organization. It was a great organization.

I found out later that they had plans for me to be a player-coach and take care of the smaller guys on Hull-Otawa because they were dynamite, but they were small. The one year, they had eleven guys who went to the National Hockey League.

So I was there, and I didn't know these plans, and one night I went out with a buddy named Claude Dufour and we went out and had a few pops, and Sammy Pollock, the general manager, calls me in.

He said, "Don, we sort of had plans for you here, but we understand you were out drinking last night."

"Well, Sam," I said, "I only had three or four."

He says, "Well, we don't believe in that around here, and like I said, we had plans for you and I want you to stop."

I said, "Look Sam, I can say I'm not going to have any beer and lie to you, but I've always had a couple of beers and I see nothing wrong with it."

"Well, Don," he says, "I appreciate your honesty. Come to see me tomorrow and we'll see what we can do."

So I came to see him in his office and he says, "Hold on. We've made arrangements. You're going to Spokane, Washington."

Well, I had no idea where that was. All I heard him say was Washington.

So I thought, "Oh boy, Washington! That's pretty good. That's pretty close to Hershey"—and Rose and the kids were in Hershey.

I says, "I didn't know Washington had a team in the American Hockey League."

He said it again: "*Spokane*, Washington."

"Man," I says. "Where's that?"

He says, "Three thousand miles away."

So we all get in the car. We loaded up our 1960 Pontiac. It was a two-door Laurentian—it was a beauty. Tim hadn't been born then. Cindy was in the back with all the clothes. We were like gypsies.

On the way out, I used to tell Cindy, "Look for the natives here." We were goin' through the deserts and all that. We had a grand time.

AL'S NOTE: *Sam Pollock is arguably the best general manager in hockey history. He joined the Montreal Canadiens organization in 1947 and became general manager in 1962. In his fourteen years as GM of the Canadiens, the team won nine Stanley Cups. One of his better deals was to trade a pair of prospects, Guy Allen and Paul Reid, to the Bruins for a young college goalie. Neither Allen nor Reid ever played in the NHL. The college goalie did. His name was Ken Dryden. Pollock was inducted into Hockey's Hall of Fame in 1978 and died in August 2007 at the age of eighty-one.*

If you covered that team, as I did, you rarely saw Sam. He was not one for hogging the limelight. But if things ever started going badly, which was a rarity with that team, there would be Sam, hanging around the dressing room after the game. He would always show up to take the heat, but he was never there to take the credit.

* * *

We finally got there, and let me tell you somethin', boy. We had a defence!

Brian Williams was told by Sammy Pollock when he interviewed him one time that the meanest team and the toughest defence ever was the four guys that played for Spokane: Sandy "Stone Face" Hucul, Bill "The Destroyer" Shvetz and Connie "Mad Dog" Madigan. Boy oh boy, were they tough! We used to have guys hurt in practice!

Spokane had a big "S" on the front of their sweaters, and when they had one of these defence pairs come at 'em, they'd say, "Here comes the SS."

We missed out on the playoffs 'cause of five-minute majors. And we had a pretty good team, too.

So I got there, and I was only there two days when we had to go on the road.

Well, the trainer was a pretty good guy and he gave me a brand new pair of gloves. I knew I was in trouble right away because I was expected to fight a little anyhow. No fighter wants new gloves. You want broken-in extra-large gloves. You give one quick shake of your hands and they're off. But I didn't want to complain about things like gloves my first game. Big mistake.

So we get to San Francisco, in the Cow Palace, and there's a big sign, sixty feet across, saying, "Larry McNab, heavyweight champion of the WHL."

"Oh no!" I've got these new gloves. I should have changed the gloves. Anyhow, sure enough, we get into it and I can't get the gloves off and I get tied up again by the linesmen. They were always tying me up. Boy, I got hit so many times when I was tied up. So we were down on our hands and knees somehow and I knew what he was trying to do: he was trying to get at my face. So I put my head down low and he was literally bouncin' his fist off the ice, trying to get at my head. He hit me so many times in the head, I couldn't comb my hair for a month. And I had hair back then.

But I fixed him. He broke his hand on my head and he was out for six weeks!

AL'S NOTE: *The fourth tough guy on this defence was, of course, Don "Baby Face" Cherry.*

Brian Williams is one of Canada's elite sports announcers, and as of 2008, he and Don had collaborated for twenty-four years on Don's daily radio show, Grapeline.

* * *

I became buddies with one of the guys on the team. He was a single guy. Tough as nails.

One year, it was Christmas morning, he came up to visit me and he brought a bottle. I never drank hard stuff, but he brought it anyhow.

On the way, he stopped at the apartment right next to us, which was another teammate's. He stopped in this place and he knocked on the door. He just wanted to come in because he was single and he had nobody to stay with, so when the door opened, he says, "Hi. How are ya doin'? Merry Christmas. Here's a bottle for ya."

The guy says, "Yeah, same to you." He took the bottle and closed the door.

Well, the guy went insane. Well, imagine! It was Christmas mornin'. So now he comes to our door and he was so mad, he was cryin'.

He said, "Can you imagine him doin' that to me? Well, I'll fix him."

We asked him to stay for Christmas dinner.

He said, "No, I'm leaving."

He was still mad. He said, "I'll get him. You watch. I'll get him."

About a week later, we're practising, and he reminded me of Larry Zeidel. He took his stick and he swung it like an axe. He hit the guy across the face and knocked all his teeth out. The guy started to hemorrhage. It was so bad, they had to get an ambulance.

They had towels wrapped around his head and the blood was comin' through the towels. They had to take him to the hospital.

So on the way home after practice, my buddy and I stopped in and we're sittin' having a beer. The five o'clock news was on TV and they showed the guy being wheeled out to go to the hospital and all the blood.

My buddy finished his beer and turned to me, and I looked at him, and I couldn't believe it. He says, "Well, I guess next Christmas, he'll invite me in for a drink."

* * *

I was sitting in the same bar with the same guy about halfway through the season. Rose had gone home to have Timothy, my son, and so I'm afraid to say I did a lot of drinkin' in the afternoon. What else was there to do?

The bar was empty. It was Steve's Smoke Shop. There were just the two of us in there and the bartender . . . Bill Ryan—I remember his name.

So we're sittin' there lookin' at TV and havin' a pop, just the two of us at a big, long bar.

So my buddy finishes his drink and goes to the washroom, and I'm just sittin' there alone lookin' at TV when this great big guy come in. I found out later, he was the military police. He comes in and sits where my buddy was sittin'.

You gotta realize there was about thirty empty seats at the bar, and my buddy comes back and taps the guy on the shoulder and says, "That's my seat."

The big guy says, "Wait a minute. What do you mean this is your seat? Sit over there."

My buddy says, "No. That's my seat. Move." I could see he was lookin' for trouble.

The guy wouldn't move. You had to see the fight to believe it. It was like somethin' out of a movie. Underneath the tables. The tables were flying. The chairs were goin'. I thought I was watchin' a Tom Mix movie.

They were going at it like you couldn't believe, so finally the big guy has got my buddy down and he's got him by both arms. The big guy looks at me, but I don't want to get involved.

My buddy says to the guy, "You'd better kill me, because if I get up, I'm going to kill you."

Finally, the big guy says, "What am I gonna do?"

I knew that if this kept up, the cops were gonna come, so I get down and I grab my buddy by the arms and I'm holding him down and I said to the big guy, "You get out of here."

I couldn't hold him much longer. I had a death grip on him. I'm holdin' him against the wall and he had tears in his eyes. He looked like he had gone insane now.

I said, "Now take it easy. I'm only holdin' you. You don't want to go to jail. The cops are gonna come. Look what you've done to the bar."

And I just knew as I held him against the wall that he was gonna knee me in the groin. I turned sideways. I tell ya, I had a death grip on him. You shoulda seen the bruises on him the next day.

Finally, he said, "Okay, Grapes, let me go." He says, "Let me go. I won't do anything. I promise. But I'm gonna tell ya. If you ever get involved in another fight I'm in, I'm gonna kill ya."

And you know what? I think he would.

* * *

One time we were in the old Vancouver arena on the Pacific Exhibition grounds. The game ended and I knew my buddy had been having a little feud with this guy during the game. So we're goin' off, both teams, and all of a sudden, I look over—and nobody has seen it, but this guy is layin' on the ice, all curled up.

I think, "What the heck is goin' on?"

So my buddy, as he's goin' by, he says, "Yeah, I just gave him the caterpillar treatment."

What he had done, when nobody was lookin', he had took his stick and drove it into the guy's stomach. I mean, I don't know, I thought *I* was tough until I saw these guys.

Sammy Pollock was right. He said these were the toughest, most vicious guys ever—and Sammy had seen them all.

Sammy don't lie.

AL'S NOTE: *The caterpillar treatment is so named because, after it has been administered, the victim is lying curled up in a ball like a caterpillar. It's rarely fatal, but it could be. In the six-team era, Doug Harvey of the Montreal Canadiens administered it to Red Sullivan of the New York Rangers, who required emergency surgery to have his spleen removed. Last rites were accorded, but Sullivan recovered and resumed his NHL career.*

* * *

One day, I had Mike Milbury, Stan Jonathan and John Wensink over. We'd had a few pops. We had a great meal from Kowloon's, if you know it. That's a great spot down there. And we had dry ribs. Boy, were they good!

And we're eatin' them and I kept tellin' the stories about Blue and I said, "You know, after a whistle, don't ever look away when you hit a guy. Look at the guy and say, 'What are you going to do about it?' If that guy looks away, you've won the fight.

"For instance," I said, "if I stare in the eyes of Blue here, who's waitin' to get a piece of meat, she'll come at me."

Well, I'd never ever tried it, eh? You know how it is. You have a few pops and you kind of go a little stupid sayin' things. I thought, "What if she doesn't? These are my players."

Anyway, I took the meat and I stared at her. Then all of a sudden, I swear, her eyes changed, like, "What the hell are you starin' at? Oh, yeah?" And she growled and was gonna come at me.

I said, "See what I mean?"

She never let me down.

Moments to live forever. We had just beat the St. Boniface Canadiens of the West for the Memorial Cup. Good looking guy third from the left, eh?

We had just beat T.O. Marlies for the OHA in the T.O. Gardens. Next visiting the Citadelles on our march to the Memorial Cup. That's me below Hap.

Gentleman Eddie Sanford (left) who showed me how to act like a hockey player at training camp. My boyhood hero Lorne Ferguson (right). I'll never forget how kind he was to me my rookie camp with Boston.

My rookie training camp.

Me as a Rochester American. I am by now a confirmed minor-leaguer.

The look of a "hard-rock" minor-leaguer. Above my right eye is two
stitches. The bone where the stitches are is permanently swollen from
the cuts and bangs I got. The skin is thin from all the cuts, and it
seemed I had cuts there from October to May. These stitches are almost
healed, and Rose will be taking them out with the cuticle scissors. When
I first met Rose she was disgusted with these cuts. But I had so many,
over four hundred in my face (How could I look so pretty?), and to save
time going to the doctor Rose learned to take the stitches out. In fact, it
seemed she enjoyed taking the stitches out. When I would squirm
because it hurt, she'd say, "Hold still, you big baby."

Terry "Taz" O'Reilly in a dust-up with a good guy who played for the Colorado Rockies, Mike Christie. Terry never liked to talk about fights after. He never started a fight, but he sure finished them.

Ralph Mellanby was the executive producer of *Hockey Night in Canada*, was named Canada's Broadcaster of the Year, won five Emmy Awards, and worked on coverage of at least twelve Olympic Games, but most important, discovered me. Gerry Patterson who showed me the way. When I came from Colorado and was having a tough time, Gerry got me started on *Grapeline* and many other things, he was a good friend. And of course, the great No. 9, Gordie Howe, giving Gerry one of his famous elbows.

Celebrating Terry O'Reilly scoring the O.T. goal at 1 a.m. in the semi-finals in Philly.

Me telling Hall of Famer, All-Star, and our leading point guy, Jean Ratelle, how to take a face-off. He's looking at me as if to say "You can't be serious." No wonder he's laughing.

John "Wire" Wensink at training camp. Notice the loose gloves and it wasn't because he wanted to shake hands. John scored 28 goals that year, he was the Ultimate Enforcer. He looked like and was a dangerous guy.

My triumphant return to Boston Garden: One of the great Boston fans had tossed these grapes. We won 5–4, what a feeling to beat Boston in Boston, with the fans hollering "Cherry, Cherry," and a standing ovation. But as usual I can't leave well enough alone. Instead of enjoying the moment, I got to ruin it. Acting the show-off with about a minute to go, I call a time out, and a kid asked me to sign an autograph, why not? So I sign autographs during a time out, ticking off Boston players, who I love, Harry Sinden, that's okay, my owners, and the fans, but what hurt the most was my son, Tim, who was fifteen and traveling with us as a stick boy, he asked after the game, "Why do you do things like that, Dad?" I wish I knew.

Phil and Bobby: The last hurrah in Boston Garden. See story on p. 16.

* * *

It was the afternoon of a game in Calgary between the Spokane Comets and Calgary. We're in the elevator—three players—and on the way down, two girls get in.

Well, the girls are laughin' and gigglin' and we know what's happening. They've come from some players' rooms. Let's say they were not the nicest girls.

We don't say nothin'. We're on the way down and one guy there was very sensitive about his hair. He wore a fedora and he was bald.

One of the girls grabbed his hat and lifted it up and says, "Look, Sue, another baldy."

Well, she embarrassed the guy. He was a good guy and, like I said, he was a very sensitive guy.

So I said to them, "Well, girls, that's the way the world is. That's nature. He's bald and he can't help it. It's like you. You're pigs and you can't help it."

* * *

Now it's game night. We're at the game. Same guy. Tie game. Gives the puck away for the winnin' goal. Those things happen.

So we're puttin' our equipment away after the game. What you do in the minor leagues, the trainer puts the bag in front of you, and as you're taking the equipment off, you put it in the bag. Well, this guy is sittin' beside me and he starts throwin' the equipment around, throwin' it in his bag. He's close to tears.

I say to him, "Take it easy. What's the matter with you? Take it easy. It happens to all of us."

But it didn't make any difference. He started to holler "I did this" and "I did that."

Boy, I'd never seen anybody like this before.

The coach, he come in and he looked at the guy, and as he went by, he said, "What happened?"

The guy went insane. I've never seen anything like it in my life. He was throwin' his equipment around and cryin' and screamin' and grabbin' his head.

I was told after that he had a nervous breakdown. They took him away and I never, ever saw him again.

* * *

The Spokane Comets were not a good team to play for if you were a sensitive guy.

For the Spokane Comets, believe me, you had to be up more for the practices than for the games.

It was the two Irish guys, Cornelius Patrick Madigan and myself, against the two Ukrainians or Polish guys—I never knew what they were, but they sure weren't Irish—Hucul and Shvetz.

It's one thing to be tough. It's another thing to *look* tough, and believe me, these three guys were the toughest-lookin' guys I've ever seen in my life. Me, I looked like Little Lord Fauntleroy beside them.

I remember I'd be havin' breakfast before goin' to practice and I'd be eatin' my eggs and gettin' ready, and Rose would say, "I don't know what it is, but you seem to be more nervous about goin' to practices than to the games."

I said, "Rose, it's hard to explain."

* * *

Even though it's a few years ago now, I remember one practice like it was yesterday. I was cutting across the blue line with my head down like a fool—in the trolley tracks, as they say.

As I did it, I knew I was in trouble. I look up, and here comes Sandy Hucul. I know I'm for it and I know I'm gonna be hurtin'. Okay, I'm ready.

Oh no! He goes by and lets me off the hook and smiles.

The humiliation of it all! Shvetz looked at me and smiled. Connie is ticked off that I could be so stupid. That puts them one up on us.

It's the only time any of those guys let anyone off the hook, and it's got to be me! For shame.

It was funny in the dressing room. Connie and I sat on one side and Shvetz and Hucul sat on the other. It's not as if we hated one another. It was just to show how tough we were.

I often hear about guys doin' this, but it was the first time I've ever seen it or been involved.

To tell you the truth, I wasn't too crazy about doin' it, but I had to go along with Connie or my life would never be the same again.

We'd be bending over, doin' up our skates, and Connie would be sayin', "Come on now, get ready. Get ready. We gotta get ready. Come on now."

It was like we were goin' to war.

I know as you read this, you're thinkin', "These guys were crazy," and maybe you're right. There might have been a little cog bent, but it was our way of life. I have to admit that it was exciting and I looked forward to it.

* * *

A lot of people wonder why so many hockey people, including me, want to get rid of the instigator rule.

If you go back to its beginning, the governors put it in—people who don't know anything about hockey. The nearest they've been to ice is the stuff in their drinks. The idea was they didn't want the tough guys pickin' on the stars.

Well, first of all, no tough guy ever picks on the stars. He just picks on the little rats that pick on the stars, as everybody knows— everybody except NHL governors at that time.

So they put in the instigator rule, and the way it works now, as Stevie Yzerman said, you can have these little guys with visors running around cross-checking and sticking and doin' everything they want, and there's no retaliation.

They get a free ride, and it's too bad, because stars now are not protected.

* * *

Back in Wayne Gretzky's day and Mike Bossy's day, it was different.

People who didn't know hockey used to say, "There's a rule. Don't tell me there isn't a rule that you can't hit Gretzky."

They said that 'cause Gretzky never got hit. Oh, I shouldn't say that. There was one guy that hit him. His name was Billy McCreary Jr. He was a distant relation to the referee Billy McCreary.

Billy Jr. played for the Toronto Maple Leafs. It was a Saturday night and I'm doing the colour on *Hockey Night in Canada*, and Gretzky was gettin' careless because nobody had ever hit him.

He reached back, cutting along the blue line, and McCreary come along and hit him head-on and knocked him cold. It was unbelievable. I kinda felt bad, because I'd kinda criticized Gretzky until then, and here he is layin' there.

Finally, he gets up. The guys told me he was on the bench goin', "Sammy! Sammy!" That's what they called Dave Semenko.

The funny thing about Billy McCreary is that he finished the shift, got off the ice and he never ever got back on the ice, because Joe Crozier was the coach of the Leafs and Crozier knew what would happen to him.

So did everyone else. When McCreary returned to the bench, Leafs defenceman Ian Turnbull said, "What are you trying to do? Get us all killed?"

Crozier knew that for McCreary's own good, he couldn't put him back on the ice.

McCreary never played another shift in the National Hockey League after kayoing Gretzky.

The real story was, as all the hockey people know, that the No-Hit

Rule—all it was—was Dave Semenko and Marty McSorley. If you tried anything at all with Gretzky, or even looked sideways at him, Semenko was there and McSorley was there.

AL'S NOTE: *The Bill McCreary Jr. in this story is one of a notable hockey family from Sundridge, Ontario. His father and his uncle Keith McCreary also played in the National Hockey League. In fact, Scott Bowman said that Bill Sr. was the best junior player he had ever seen. As a fifteen-year-old he played junior hockey for the Guelph Biltmores on a line with Dean Prentice and Andy Bathgate.*

Bill Sr. played eight seasons in the NHL and went to the Stanley Cup final three times with the St. Louis Blues. At some points in his minor-league career, he played against Don.

As Don said, Bill Jr. never played another NHL shift after hitting Gretzky. The Leafs sent him to their Cincinnati farm team the next day and he was subsequently traded to the Chicago Blackhawks. He spent a year in their minor-league system before leaving hockey and getting into the insurance business, where he has been very successful and remains to this day.

Bill Jr.'s grandfather is the brother of NHL referee Bill McCreary's father.

* * *

I remember when I coached Colorado. A beautiful guy by the name of Ronnie Delorme, who's the chief scout for Vancouver now, he hit Gretzky by accident. It was one of those deals where they were looking the other way and ran into each other. The Oilers were trying to come in the bench and get him!

Ronnie was saying, "I didn't mean to hit him! It was an accident." You should know, though, that Ronnie didn't care. He'd fight the world.

But Gretzky was protected. He had the protection, and the one time he really got hurt was when he played for Team Canada and Gary Suter hit him into the boards from behind and hurt his back.

I guarantee you Suter would not have done that in an NHL game with Semenko and McSorley around.

Suter was the same guy that cross-checked Paul Kariya after a goal and gave him a concussion. Remember that? They went out and got Jim McKenzie after that—after Kariya said, "You gotta get a tough guy in here to protect us."

It's so sad. It's so sad because the guy that comes in to protect, under the instigator rule, gets a two-minute minor, a five-minute major and ten-minute misconduct. And he's not the guy who initiated it. It's some little rat doin' it. Worse still, if you do it in the last five minutes of the game, which is often a good time to get even, you get a one-game suspension.

It was the same thing with Mike Bossy. When Bossy played, he had Clark Gillies and Bob Nystrom. You touched Bossy and they were comin'. So it's a sad, sad situation that we have now.

We had a beautiful thing going. I compare it to a forest, and in this forest, everybody gets along. You've got the tiger, you've got the deer, you've got the hyenas. The hyenas were always circling around on the outside because they were afraid of the tigers. They would never come in the forest and everybody got along great, and down by the drinking pond, everything was good.

But somebody said, "Oh, let's get rid of those big, bad tigers."

Sure enough, they got rid of the tigers, and guess what moved in? The hyenas. That's what I call the guys who stick and are pests.

They've got to get the instigator rule out. In fact, in *The Hockey News*, the players had a vote. They were asked what's the three dumb rules you'd get out? Well, first of all, it was the instigator rule. Number one.

Number two was flipping the puck over the glass—another dumb penalty of all time. I called that one. I said before the first season with that rule, "That's gonna cost someone a series." It cost Montreal a series. It cost Buffalo a series. It seems they always score on that penalty.

And of course, the other one the players want out is touch-icing. I'll talk about that one later.

The instigator rule should be taken out. It hurts hockey. Before, the stars were protected. They could do anything they wanted. Now, it's open season on our stars.

* * *

It was 1982. I got a call from an executive producer at the CBC. They wanted Bob Cole and me to fly out to LA to do a game between Edmonton and LA in the playoffs.

It looked like Edmonton was smokin' everybody, and it was gonna be a nothing game, another runaway for Edmonton.

So Bob Cole and me went out. I don't think many people were watchin'. I don't even know if it was on back east or not.

So as usual, Edmonton ran up the score and it was 5–0. It was embarrassing to watch.

Edmonton was killin' a penalty and Dave Lumley, one of the Edmonton penalty killers, was talking to the LA players on the bench, saying, "You call this a power play?"

The Kings' owner, Dr. Jerry Buss, sat right down by the glass and he had a beautiful blonde with him. He was so disgusted, he got up to leave, and Bob said, "There goes Dr. Buss."

I said, "Well, Bob, if he's got to leave, he's leavin' with a beauty."

Everybody thought the game was over. LA got a goal, but so what? It's 5–1. It doesn't make much difference.

Then they got a second. Aw, it's only 5–2. They're not gonna do anything with Grant Fuhr in the net and Gretzky, Messier, all these guys playin' for Edmonton—not a chance.

Then they make it 5–3. Hmmm. I think it's getting a little dicey here now. But still, 5–3 with Fuhr. Shouldn't be a problem.

Now it's 5–4! They've popped in another one. Now it's panic time for Edmonton.

I mean, you talk about panic! They're running all over. And now it's 5–5.

I never saw a game like this. It was called the Miracle on

Manchester Street. John Shannon said it was the greatest game he ever saw.

Now it's in overtime. It's a faceoff in the Edmonton end. Right-hand side. Doug Smith is a left-hand draw. He beats Messier cleanly and pulls it back to Darryl Evans.

He puts it top corner. A slapshot like you wouldn't believe. They run and jump on each other. They run and they're sliding towards the goalpost. I've never seen anything like that before. If they'd have hit it, somebody would've been seriously hurt.

I never saw a game like that before or since. It's 5–0 and guys are jerking around saying, "You call this a power play?"

And look what happened.

* * *

Now they go back to Edmonton for game five, and I remember Ron MacLean and I were doing the openin' on the ice, and you could see LA could hardly wait to get the game goin'. I remember Marcel Dionne goin' by us when we were on the ice. He winked at me. He said, "We're gonna get these guys."

Sure enough, they beat them, and as Gretzky said after, this was the biggest lesson he and the Edmonton team ever learned. Don't get too cocky when you're up.

They learned their lesson, and from then on, they were the best team in the league. They lost to the Islanders in the final the year after, then won five of the next seven Stanley Cups.

But the Miracle on Manchester Street—many guys say they've never seen anything like it before or since.

And the funny thing was, when Bob Cole and I went out there, we thought it was gonna be just another game. It was one of the greatest games I've ever seen.

AL'S NOTE: *In that era, the first-round series was a best-of-five affair. The teams split the first two games in Edmonton, and the Miracle on*

Manchester was game three. The Oilers stayed alive by winning 3–2 in game four, but lost game five at home, 7–4.

It was the biggest playoff upset in history. The Oilers had 111 points in the regular season, compared to 63 for the Kings. In the eight regular-season meetings, the Kings won only once and were outscored 51–27.

* * *

It was January 4, 1987, and I get a call that I was supposed to go down to the CBC and help Brian Williams with the World Junior Championship. It wasn't *Hockey Night in Canada* calling, it was CBC.

Well, I didn't really want to go. I just didn't feel like it.

The fact is, I had a hangover to start with. Besides, the NFL play-offs were on and I figure who the heck is going to be watching the CBC when the NFL playoffs are on?

Also, it was kinda dicey whether Canada would win, but if they won this game and the next game, they'd win the gold.

So the game's going along pretty good and Canada's winning, and it's near the end of the first period. All of a sudden, I look up and all the Russians come on the ice. Well, everybody knows why the Russians come on the ice. They had no chance of winning the gold. Canada had a good chance.

The Russians watched to see if they were gonna get beat, and they were. The coach sent everybody on.

Well, the Canadian coach was Bert Templeton, and what's he gonna do? Pat Burns was the assistant coach. What's he gonna do? Are they gonna hold their guys there while twenty guys beat up six? So out they go.

It's the first time in my life—and I've been through hockey for a million games—that I've seen *every* guy goin' at it. I understand the Canadian trainer punched out their trainer. Even the backup goalies were goin' at it.

And if you remember, they couldn't stop it. The referees just skated off the ice.

Then they turned off the lights.

Brendan Shanahan told me after, "You should have seen what we were doin' while the lights were out."

So they finally get broke up and Brian Williams, who's the host of the CBC show, comes on and says, "It's a black mark. These boys have to learn that they can not be hoodlums." And he's goin' on like that.

I understand that one of the team executives went in and gave it to them in the dressing room after, and the kids were crying. And I have to say that the three guys who were doin' the broadcast and the colour didn't stick up for them, either.

So I says, "What the hell? I've been on television long enough, I guess," so I'm gonna go down swingin'.

So Brian's goin' on about it bein' a black mark and a disgrace and I turned to him and said, "Look, if you don't send those kids on the ice, what are you gonna do? Are you gonna let twenty Russians beat up six Canadians?"

I went on like that. I thought I was finished, 'cause you're not supposed to say that kids should be sent out to beat up other kids and stuff like that. The CBC was a little touchy at the time.

When we went away for a break, I said, "Brian, if you say about these kids one more time that it's a black mark against them—you say it one more time—and I'm gonna grab you right on television."

He knew I was serious, so he moved his seat.

* * *

So the cameraman thought I was kiddin' and he says, "When we come back, why don't you have your hands around Brian's throat?"

I said, "No, I'd better not. Because if I do, I wouldn't let go of the little son of a bitch."

When we came back, Brian was very guarded. We got through it.

We ran the fight again and I said that if Bert Templeton hadn't sent them on, he wouldn't have been a man. You don't stand by and see twenty Russians beat up six Canadians.

So as I'm leavin' the building, there was a producer, a guy with long, white hair who's still hangin' around there. I had to go right behind him, and as I'm doin' it, he says, "You're finished on television."

I said "Good. I don't need it. Who the **** cares?" I thought I was done.

* * *

So you must realize that Rose always gave me heck about what I did on television. Everything I did seemed to be wrong, because she hated to see me act the way I do.

So I'm goin' home, and I'm drivin' along and I figure, "Oh, the radio's gonna give it to me and Rose is gonna give it to me."

So I get home and I'm taking off my coat and she starts, "If that Brian Williams ever says anything like that again . . ." and she's hot at Brian. She's really hot at Brian!

And I'm thinkin', "Whoa, if Rose is hot at Brian, how about the rest of the country?"

Five minutes later, the phone rings and it's Brian Williams. He's in tears.

Rose answers it and he says, "I don't know what I did! My kids come home and they say, 'What are we, Communists, Dad? The other kids are givin' us heck and tellin' us we're Communists and everybody's yellin at us.'"

Then he starts talking about himself. He says, "They're gonna get me. I'm gonna have to get out of town. I can't believe the reaction against me. What has Don done?"

So Rose put her hand over the mouthpiece and hands me the phone and says, "It's Brian. You be kind to him. Don't you antagonize him anymore."

I says, "I won't, Rose."

So she gives me the phone and I said, "Hello, Comrade, how you doin'?"

* * *

There was a guy on the radio and he was givin' it to me pretty good.

We had kind of a conversation goin' on, but he was against what the kids had done.

So finally I said to him, "Do you have a son?"

"Yes."

"If you were walking along the street with your son and three guys jumped him, and started to beat him up, wouldn't you go in to help him?"

He said, "No, I'd phone the police."

I said, "I don't want to talk to this guy anymore."

* * *

A little epilogue to this, as they say. Or a postscript.

Some time afterwards, I was at a Mississauga sports banquet, and Brian was in the audience. I says, "Ladies and gentlemen, I just want you to know that we have a celebrity here—Brian Williams—and that Brian paid his way to get in."

Everybody kinda clapped. A little bit. Not much, because they were still mad at him.

I said, "Brian, how much did it cost in rubles to get in here?"

Well, he wasn't too happy.

I said, "Yes, ladies and gentlemen. I knew he was here because I saw his Lada parked outside."

He was even less happy about that.

* * *

I'm often asked if the players ever come to the games drunk. I can honestly say I've never, ever seen a guy come to the game drunk.

I know I've heard of it in the minor leagues, but I've never seen it, and I've played in every league that existed. I played in the American league, the Central league, the Western league, the Eastern Pro league and one game in the National Hockey League.

So I've never seen it, but I've seen guys come to practice so hung over that they're still drunk. A lot of people don't realize that when you're drunk—not really so hammered that you can't walk and that, but with a real bad hangover—you're still half-drunk. In that condition, when you're skating forward, you can do pretty good.

But a lot of people don't know that you can't skate backwards if you're still half-cut. It just can't happen.

Well, when I was coaching Boston, we were in Atlanta one time and I had one of my players come into the morning skate like that. He was doin' pretty good, but I knew. I blew the whistle and said, "Okay, backwards now."

He kept fallin', kept fallin'. The players didn't laugh or anything because they thought I was really gonna give it to him. But he was a veteran. I went up to him and I said, "You're not feelin' too well, right?"

He says, "No."

I says, "You've got the flu, right? Remember, you've got the flu."

The general manager was coming to watch the practice. If he'd have saw this, this guy would have been in deep trouble.

So he went in to the room and I said, "Tell the trainer you've got the flu. I'll let you have the flu this time, but don't ever, *ever* have that flu again and put a show on like this again. Got it?"

You know what? He never did for the next five years.

* * *

There's no question at all about the best trade I was ever involved in.

It was the one that saved my job. It was my second year coaching in Boston and we were going nowhere. Bobby was hurt. We were absolutely going nowhere, and I remember Harry came to me, saying, "Would you trade Phil Esposito and Dallas Smith for Brad Park and Jean Ratelle?"

I said, "Are you kiddin'? In a minute." Like I said we were dead in the water.

We had a little snag. Harry worked on it and worked on it. The Rangers didn't want Dallas Smith. They wanted Carol Vadnais.

Carol Vadnais, I'd have to say, was one of my best friends on the team—which might seem a little strange, but he was. I really didn't want to do anything with Vad, but I thought, "Well, we'd better do somethin' because we're goin' down fast."

We were flying out to Vancouver when this trade was in the works pretty good, and we're out at the airport, and I remember Phil standin' there and eatin' a bun or a muffin or somethin'. He says, "You know, Grapes, I'm gonna start playing the way you want me to play."

What he meant by that was he was used to stayin' on the ice for two or three minutes, and I wanted him to come off the ice after one minute. I don't think Phil ever changed on the fly in his life.

Andre Savard used to be the next centre up after Phil all the time, and he'd sit there with one leg over the boards, waitin' for Phil to come off. I told him, "Andy, if you ever get married, you won't have any children sittin' there like that all the time."

The deal was close, but it didn't go through, so we land in Vancouver and I get a call early in the morning. I'd say it was about 6:30 in the morning. It was Harry.

He says, "The deal has gone through. They took Vadnais and Phil for Park, Ratelle and Joe Zanuzzi, a minor leaguer." Joe called himself the biggest spare wheel in the world. He was a good guy.

Anyway, Harry says, "You've got to get to Phil quick because the papers are going to hit pretty soon. Somehow, it leaked out, and you don't want the papers to phone him first."

Phil always said that I favoured Bobby—"Bobby this, Bobby that," he said. "I get sixty-five goals."

He wasn't really jealous. He was just kiddin'. But I did favour Bobby. Who wouldn't?

But I figured I'd better take Bobby along, and after Harry called, I call Bobby, and Bobby meets me in the hall a little after 6:30 in the morning. He had shorts and a T-shirt on. We knock on the door and Phil answers the door.

He's in white silk pajamas, if you can believe it.

Afterwards, he told me that when he saw me at the door, he thought that I had been fired. Surprise, surprise, Phil.

We walk in. Now he knows it's serious. Bobby goes over and stands at the window. He's really ticked. He's Phil's buddy and they've been through a lot. He's ticked and he's looking out the window. It's raining.

I said, "Phil, you've been traded." He got all teary-eyed and choked up.

Phil says, "Grapes, if you tell me I've been traded to the New York Rangers, I'm jumpin' out that window."

I said, "Bobby, get away from that window." It wasn't funny, I guess, but at the time it seemed funny.

So Phil accepted it. What was he gonna do?

* * *

So now I go to Carol Vadnais's room. He was rooming with Gary Doak. Come to think of it, Phil was rooming alone.

I said, "Gary, would you take a walk, please?"

I told Vad he was traded.

Vad said, "My wife, Raymonde, is not well. She's been in and out of the hospital and now this happens."

I said, "Well, Vad, that's the way it is."

He says, "Wait a minute! I can't be traded. I've got a no-trade contract!"

I says, "Well, I don't think Harry would do that."

Vad says, "I'm telling you, Grapes, I've got a no-trade contract."

So, right from his room, I phone Harry and I says, "Harry, I'm with Vad and he says he has a no-trade contract."

Harry says, "Oh, no. That's not true."

But I can hear him flippin' pages, and all of a sudden, things go silent. So I wait for a couple of minutes and I say, "Harry? Harry?"

I know he's still there because you can tell if someone's still on the line, so it looked as if Vad had a no-trade contract.

It worked out, because I think Vad got an extra $100,000 to ignore the no-trade clause and go, and he was the toast of New York while he was there. It was sad, though, because I really liked those two guys. Still, that's the way the world is.

* * *

Later that morning, we have a practice in Vancouver, and Phil—I wish he hadn't done it—he goes around and shakes hands with everybody sitting on their bench in the dressing room. He's teary-eyed again. I'll tell ya, it was an emotional time for everybody.

Then I go out on the ice and blow the whistle and I say, "Let's go," and I have a mutiny! They won't even speak. Bobby come up to me and he says, "Were you part of that trade?"

I says, "I sure was."

He was really ticked. He says, "Why didn't you wait?"

Now everybody's ticked and nobody's skatin'. Anyhow, I call them over and I said, "Listen you ****ing guys. Yeah, they're gone. I'm gonna blow this ****ing whistle and if you don't skate, there's gonna be a lot more guys gone!"

Well, they picked it up and they skated. I could understand they felt bad. But Park arrived the next day and they were ready to go.

* * *

It was a kinda tough time, too, for Harry because there were big headlines in the paper. In Boston, the Bruins were big in those days. And the paper had a cartoon of Emile Francis, the Rangers' GM, as a bandit with a black mask stealing Vadnais and Phil.

And there was Harry sitting with Ratelle with a bad back—which he did have a bad back—and Park with a bad knee. And he did have a bad knee. But little did they know.

We played that night and we lost, but you could see Park and Orr. Man were they great!

So I get a call from Harry after the game and I says, "We lost, Harry, but I saw something."

He says, "You'd damn well better see somethin' or we're both gone."

Two nights later, we play in Oakland and we're winning, and Park and Orr are unbelievable. Two magicians. We're winning 5–2 and the Seals score a third goal and I'm tellin' you, I start to panic because I can see my job going down the drain.

I swear Bobby stopped back of the net and looked over at me, as if to say, "Calm down!" And he looked over at the two wingers. "Everybody calm down!" He almost was sayin' that. "Take it easy."

And that's the way it was. After that, it was unbelievable. They played the point on the power play naturally, the two of them. Park on the left side and Bobby on the right. They did a strange thing that I've never seen anybody else do. They stayed on the boards, which is amazing, but they were so good at passing the puck, they didn't have to be close to each other.

Park would just feather that puck over to Bobby and he'd let that slapshot go, that snapshot. It was unbelievable. I think between the two of them, they had ten goals in ten games and we won nine straight.

* * *

Cesare Maniago was a great goalie back then. He played for five NHL teams including the Rangers and Leafs, and he had spent a lot of time in the minors before he got his chance. He even played senior hockey before he got to the NHL.

He once said that when you're a goalie, and Bobby and Brad are on the point passing that puck back and forth, it was like sittin' there with two cannons pointed at you. And you never knew which one was going to go off.

AL'S NOTE: *Cesare Maniago was typical of goalies of his era—which included the days of the six-team league. NHL goalies didn't have backups, so jobs were scarce and goalies bounced around and waited for an opening.*

Maniago was almost as well travelled as Don. He played with Spokane and Vancouver in the Western Hockey League; Sudbury and Hull-Ottawa in the Eastern Professional Hockey League; Quebec in the American Hockey League; and Omaha, Minnesota and Baltimore in the Central Hockey League. And that was before playing for five teams over fifteen years in the NHL.

* * *

Things looked so good, I phoned my mom and I said, "We've got a Stanley Cup ring comin' for sure."

But unbeknownst to me, something was going to happen. For now, though, things are rollin'.

The game before it happened, we played the New York Rangers, and John Davidson was in the net with that big glove, and Bobby and Brad were puttin' on a show. I remember Bobby kept wiring it, and John Davidson, he was a big guy and a strong guy. He'd stop it and catch it.

And I remember Bobby one time winding up, and I'm sure he was thinking, "This puck is either goin' by you or through you," and it literally tore the glove off John Davidson's hand. We won the game 5–3. Bobby was one of the three stars. So was Park.

In Madison Square Garden, the bus parks down at the bottom and you have to walk a long ways down a tunnel. The ice surface is actually on the fifth floor, and fans get up to that level by escalators, but the players walk.

Well, if anybody has had a bad knee — and I've had a bad knee — you can walk up all night, but if you walk down, something happens to your knee.

So I'm sittin' in the front of the bus, watchin' Bobby comin' down this ramp, and I notice that near the end, he starts limpin'. And I says, "What's the matter, Bobby? Did you get hurt in the game?"

He says, "No, it just started to hurt now." I knew exactly what had happened.

Three days later, we're flyin' out to Chicago. He got on the plane and while he was on the plane, his knee locked on him. And as I started to get on the plane, they were carrying him out with his knee locked on him.

He said, "Grapes, I can't move it." I'm not ashamed to say I sat in my seat and tears rolled down.

There went my Stanley Cup, because Bobby never ever came back to play the way he was before, and I still say, it was that tunnel that he walked down. Every time I see the players walking up and down that on television, I think of Bobby and what could have been.

* * *

In Kitchener, when I was playing in the EPHL, I saw an injury I never forgot. It was so unusual, the injury. It was to a guy named Toughie Hall.

In Kitchener, they had a unique thing that was supposed to be an experiment, and it worked pretty good for a while. What it was, it was a rubber hose attached to the shower head, and it came down and inside there was a casing, of sort of a rubber canvas, that went around the knee and strapped on.

What it did was, you turned on the hot water to a certain temperature—not too hot—and you had the water flowing around the knee, and it would work pretty good. We were asked to try it out and it was working pretty good. One of the players had a sore knee. That was Toughie Hall.

Everythin' was goin' along, and I never forgot the name of the guy that flushed the toilet. It was Bobby Sabourin. The toilet was next door to the shower. When he flushed the toilet, he took all the cold water away, and boiling-hot water got into this guy's knee and it was absolutely scalding his knee.

Well, he screamed. You never heard such screams in your life. It took us a while to rip it off. You shoulda seen his knee. It was like boiled meat. Finally, the ambulance came, and I was always one of the guys—I don't know how it came about—that rode with the guys when they were injured.

And I never forgot that when he was moaning in the ambulance, it was the first time I ever heard a player who was in deep pain calling for his mother. It was like, "Mom, Mom."

And I found out later, and I've read lately, 'cause I read all these army books—not that it's the same comparison, believe me—that the soldiers do the same thing when they're badly wounded in the field. They don't shout for their wife or kids. They go for their mom.

I never, ever forgot that. Toughie Hall. And you know that with a name like Toughie, it was a bad injury. I never ever forgot him calling for his mother. I can still hear him: "Oh Mom, Mom!"

* * *

Going back to the trade of Phil Esposito and Carol Vadnais, a great guy, we got Ratelle, Park and Zanuzzi, like I said.

The first time they walked into my room, the afternoon of the

game, they had flown all day from New York and they walked in
the room in the afternoon because there was a three-hour time difference. They were ready to go.

I talked to Ratelle, and I remember I had played against him in
the minors. He was a little older by then, but he reminded me of
Jean Beliveau. He had that same class as Beliveau.

He reminded me of a priest. Sometimes I'd get into a session in
the room between periods and I'd be swearing, and I'd look at him
and I'd feel bad.

The first thing I noticed with him was that he was so thin. He
was like a racehorse, and I thought, "This has been one of his problems." On the New York Rangers, they always practised. Never days
off—morning skates, the whole deal. I said to myself, "This guy is
going to get some time off."

So, what we used to do is we used to play on the weekends, naturally, and we very rarely played Monday and Tuesday. Then we'd
play Thursday and sometimes we'd play Wednesday.

Well, I had a heck of a time. I wanted him to take Monday and
Tuesday off, 'cause he didn't need to practise. There wasn't an
ounce of fat on him. But do you think I could get him to stay home
and rest? He wouldn't go out on the ice, but he'd be there working
on his sticks and everything.

Finally, I said, "Look Jean, you know I don't want you coming to
the rink. Stay home. If anybody says anything to me about you not
coming to the rink, don't worry about it. I'll say I'm giving you a
rest or you've got the flu or whatever. You just don't worry about it.
You just stay home Monday and Tuesday."

Well, I had an awful time getting him to do it. But I finally did,
and at the end, when I called an optional practice, he never showed
up and he became our leading scorer.

He had a bad back, too, and his back was so bad that he was
a professional golfer, but he had to give up golfing. He was one
of those guys that, when you went on the road, you had to phone
ahead and say, "Put a board in the bed in his room."

But gettin' some rest was one of the reasons that he turned into our leading scorer and he played a long time.

I hate to say it. After I left, they made him practise a lot, and he didn't last too long.

* * *

Jean was one of those guys. He was the last of the Mohicans, as they say. He had a straight stick, but what a backhand he had. So I used to be on him all the time. You know, "Jean, you're doing great and I know you can do a great backhand and everything, but why don't you have just a slight curve?"

He'd say, "No, no, Donnee. I've been doing it this way a long time."

So I ordered his sticks with just a slight curve, and you could see he had a little more zing in his shots. I never mentioned it and he never mentioned it.

He won the Lady Byng, and I used to be in the dressing room between periods: "I don't want any damn Lady Byng winners on this team! There'll be no Lady Byngs on my club!"

Well, he won the Lady Byng. He thought I was serious. He was such a great guy he come in my office and said he was sorry he won the Lady Byng.

What a guy! The guys loved him. He was father-like. He was so quiet and so nice, but they used to play tricks on him. As soon as the winter started, he'd put those rubbers on his shoes. Just half-rubbers. But he'd never take them off.

So, Bobby Schmautz and the guys went and got glue and glued them on. I would have liked to have seen it at the end of the season when he tried to take them off.

* * *

At that time, they were just startin' to have women hockey reporters, and the first one was in New York. Well, she was a girl reporter, actually, and they had her come in the room when the guys were naked.

I was so embarrassed. There's the guys walkin' around naked and she's got a notebook. I couldn't believe it. She started to talk to me, and I said, "Can we go outside? This is embarrassing."

She said, "Well, no. This doesn't embarrass me."

I said, "Well, it embarrasses *me*."

The same thing happened in Boston. We had a woman reporter who wanted to go into the room all the time and she'd go in. Finally, Jean Ratelle came to me and said, "I refuse to go into the dressing room anymore. I will not put up with a woman in the dressing room."

He really *was* a priest!

The girl wanted to interview Jean, and I said, "Listen, you can interview anyone you want. I'll give you my office. You just name it and Jean will be here and he'll have his robe on and you can interview him."

She wasn't happy, but she went along with it.

* * *

The guys loved Jean so much and the word got out: You touch Jean Ratelle and you're going to be a dead man. He was like our Gretzky. The word got around: Don't touch him at any time, no matter what the score was. If someone went and cross-checked him or hurt him, it was going to be six months in the hospital or six feet under.

Well, we had three games left in the 1976–77 season and we were going for first spot. We were in a dogfight with Buffalo for the first spot in the division and we're playin' on the Island.

The score was 2–2 — and it would have to have been in the second period — and they had a guy named Gerry Hart. He had long, blond, curly hair and he was not very tall, but he was a stocky defenceman and he cross-checked Jean — Ratty, as the guys used to call him.

John Wensink was programmed: You don't touch Ratelle.

He grabbed Hart, rammed his head into the boards and did a number on him. For some reason, he only got two minutes.

Well, some of the guys on our bench are sayin', "We're fightin' for first place. What is he doin'?"

I jumped up on the bench and shouted, "Attaboy, John! You protect Ratty! You protect our Jean. Don't you worry about it."

But really, I'm thinkin', "Holy Dinah, what are we goin' to do now?"

So I called over Davie Forbes and I called over Donnie Marcotte and I said to them, "If you ever killed a penalty, kill this one."

Well, they killed the penalty and the score is still tied in the third period and the puck come out of the corner and went on the backhand of Jean Ratelle and he put it in the top corner—a lovely backhand—and we won 3–2.

The guys loved Jean. There was no better guy that ever walked the earth than Jean Ratelle. A complete gentleman.

* * *

Carol Vadnais.

Carol and I, when we were in the airports, were always hanging around together and talking. He was a smooth, elegant French-Canadian.

I saw that when he travelled, he would wear a coat, but he wouldn't wear a suit underneath. I says, "How come?"

He says, "Well, I don't want to wrinkle my jacket. I'll carry it around in my suit bag and I'll have it look good when we get to where we're going."

I thought, "Well, that's a pretty good idea," so from then on, I had my coats made, and I wore a vest and just my coat.

I still do it to this day.

* * *

Andy Savard said, "It's the old story. When you see Vad, you see Don, and when you see Don, you see Vad."

We became good friends, and unfortunately, as you know as I said earlier, we traded him to New York. He and his wife, Raymonde, were a classy pair.

So it's 1976 and I was the assistant coach on Team Canada in the Canada Cup and he was there, so we were kinda hanging around then. It was in Montreal.

He said, "Don, I'm going to go out and get a couple of rings at my jeweller's." He used to call it "my jeweller's."

He asked me if I wanted to go, and I had nothing to do that afternoon, so I took a drive. I had won three straight Calder Cups, and Joe Crozier had given us a ring for the Calder Cups, but unfortunately, they weren't diamonds. They were glass and they did not look too good after a couple of years.

So I'm in the jeweller's. Vad's into jewellery and we're sittin' there and Vad's doin' somethin' with Raymonde's ring or somethin'. So I said to the jeweller, "You know, if I could have three little diamond chips, not too big, put into this ring, could you do that?"

And Vad says, "Give me the ring, Don," and he said something to the guy in French.

So I went back a week later by myself and I asked for the ring. The guy brought it out and there's a great big diamond in it with two medium-sized diamonds.

Well, I had no money. I didn't know what to do. I had no credit card. I couldn't afford this.

So I says to the guy, "Gee, this is beautiful, but I didn't ask for this. I asked for three little chips. I can't afford it."

The guy says, "Don't worry about it."

I says, "What do you mean, don't worry about it?"

What happened was, Vad had won the Stanley Cup with the Boston Bruins. He did not wear big rings like that. He took all the diamonds out of his ring and had a little ring made for Raymonde with the rest of the diamonds.

And what he said to the jeweller in French was, "Take the big diamond from the ring and put it with the two medium ones in Don's ring and send me the bill."

I couldn't speak. I was all choked up. Here I'd just traded the guy, and he does that for me.

Vad and Ratty: two class guys.

* * *

Every team has a guy that the coach sort of picks on. Everybody knows that the coach likes him, but he's always givin' him a shot. Mine was Bobby Miller from Billerica, Massachusetts.

He was my second American on the club. The first was Mike Milbury.

Miller was a good-lookin' guy with curly hair, and he was a stir-'em-up guy. What I mean by a stir-'em-up guy is he's not goin' to get you many goals, but he's gonna stir it up. Although he did get 20 one year.

Your first and second line, you always had them to do the scoring. Then the third and fourth line are the penalty killers and the checkers. You can't have all scorers. So Miller was on the stir-it-up line. We used to kid him all the time.

For him to make the club was pretty tough because he was not a big goal scorer and we had two rookies—Miller and another guy—going for a spot on those third and fourth lines. Harry wanted the one guy and I wanted Miller.

I hate to say it, but coaches can make a guy look good and they can make a guy look bad. I'm not saying I made the other guy look bad. He was a good guy and a good player, but he was a scorer, not a checker. I had enough scorers, I needed a checker. But I really worked on making Miller look good.

For instance, in the exhibition games all the way through the pre-season, I would play him to death and try to get him on the power play, get scores, kill the penalty. He was a good penalty killer, a good draw guy and a good checker.

It was neck and neck who was gonna make the club. It was our eighth exhibition game and it was our last one on the way home. We were playin' Hartford.

We were the first NHL team to play Hartford in Hartford and we walked in dead tired. They were still in the World Hockey Association before it merged with the NHL, and holy smokes, there were signs all over — "You're the NHL. We'll show you." "We're ready for you." "Hartford will show you" — and all that. I'm thinkin', "Oh man, how did we get into this?"

We get playin', and we weren't playin' that well, but I think we had a 6–0 lead. I played Miller to death. He would be on the bench and I'd look at Jean Ratelle and say, "Jean, how's that wrist that you banged up at the start of the second period?"

He knew what I was doin'. He knew I wanted Miller to play more. "Oh Donnee, it's not too good."

So we started the third period, and I said to Gregg Sheppard, our other top centreman, "How's that groin that's been bothering you, Shep?"

He says, "Oh, not too good, Grapes. Not very good."

So I played Miller to death. I think he had two goals and an assist, and that meant he made the club.

* * *

Miller was a guy we all had fun with.

To this day, the guys all try to look white and sick in the playoffs. It's sort of a mark of distinction that shows that you're workin' hard and you don't get tanned.

Well, Miller didn't know this and we got a bye in the first round. That's what happened if you won your division in those days.

We had a couple of days off and Miller went fishin'. He got all tanned up. I get on the plane and look back at the club and we're all white and everything like we should be, except he's all tanned up.

So I walk back and stop in front of him and say, "Hey! What is this?"

He says, "What Grapes? What?"

I says, "You're all tanned up! Look at the rest of us. What have you been doin'? Where've you been?"

He says, "Well, I didn't mean to. I went fishin'."

So I really reamed him and he says, "Well, what am I gonna do, Grapes?"

I says, "Get rid of it!"

The guys were all laughin' and poor Bobby Miller just sat there. Get rid of it!

* * *

I really enjoyed my time on ESPN in 2008. It was rather hectic to do.

Ron and I would finish the signoff for *Hockey Night in Canada*, I would race down to the corridors, the halls were full of people and guys doing TV interviews. After I worked my way through to ESPN, Steve Levy and Barry Melrose were waiting there, and we would do about four minutes.

I really appreciated Steve and Barry. They were there to help me and make me look good, which I know is real hard. But I thought it would be a thing between Barry and me because he's their guy for hockey, but no, he made me feel welcome. He never ever tried to match me in our suits and jackets. Of course he never had a chance there, but it was so good of those guys.

You know what's good about it, Ron and I would go back to the hotel room with our fourteen pops on ice, with peanuts and Ron's favourite—popcorn. While Ron is doing interviews, I'm out hustling popcorn in the arena. I got a bag of popcorn in a plastic bag. It's funny to see two so-called stars walking out with a clear plastic bag of a ton of popcorn.

So then we'd sit and watch my interviews on ESPN and then the next day it would run all day on their news and they'd really promote the interview. This is sort of a big deal because ESPN is not that big on hockey, but I'll tell ya, everybody watches ESPN; it is really big time.

We'd be in a bar in Pittsburgh and the bartenders would say, "Grapes, caught you on ESPN. Great."

Ron and I would look at each other in wonder. It's strange, since that little appearance on ESPN my mail comes from people in Tennessee, Oregon, South Virginia and Georgia who really enjoyed it and were Canadians living in the States who can't get CBC. They said it made them feel at home.

Speaking of that reminds me of a story I read about our most famous Canadian, Mike Myers. It seems he was in London, England, when he was not famous. He was in a bar called The Maple Leaf, a Canadian bar in London. He was all by himself sitting at the bar and feeling lonely and down and homesick. The bar put on CBC and the hockey game, and when "Coach's Corner" came on, he started to cry, it made him so homesick. But I digress, as MacLean would say.

It was great of Barry Melrose to treat me so good. It hasn't always been that good, in fact, he disliked me very much, and here's the story.

In hockey, a coach never ever makes fun of another coach. I was absolutely infuriated when Barry Melrose made fun of Pat Burns for bein' too fat.

It was a game between LA and Toronto in the '93 playoffs, and Marty McSorley hit Dougie Gilmour and the benches went wild. Barry, who was coaching LA, and Pat Burns, who was coaching Toronto, started hollering at one another. Barry held his belly and blew out his cheeks and made fun of Pat, as if he was fat.

Now being a little heavy myself, I took exception and proceeded to rip Barry big time. One statement I remember was, "Look at that long, greasy hair. He said he kept it long to bug his dad. What kind of a guy is that?" Barry was not happy.

Toronto is up 3–2 back in LA, Ron and I go to the morning skate. I look at the morning skate and tell Ron Toronto's not winning the series (they didn't). Ron disappears, I don't notice.

What happened was the PR guy for LA got Ron and said Barry would like to see him in the office. Ron goes down and walks through the players, goes into the office and Barry says, "I don't mind that Cherry says things about me, but when he brings my family into it, that's not fair. I want a public apology."

Ron says, "Barry, are you nuts? If Cherry even hears you called me down here your life will not be your own. He will crucify you."

What made Barry so upset, unbeknownst to me, was CBC had Barry's father and Wendel Clark's father together watching that game and hearing me give it to Barry. No wonder he was ticked off, and for a long time. But we made up at an All-Star game in Rochester. He coached one team and me another. He's a good guy and he was right, I shouldn't have brought his dad into it.

He'll do a great job in Tampa.

※ ※ ※

We were in Vancouver one time, and we were in there for three or four days. I gotta admit, I'd let the guys party sometimes—as long as they don't wreck the room and as long as they don't get arrested.

This one time, you couldn't believe the party we had. The guys got all loosened up and we had a great time. That was Thursday night and we didn't play until Saturday.

But we still had to practise Friday, and unbeknownst to me, the Vancouver coach said, "We're going to take some of our younger players down to see the Bruins practise." We were in first place by about ten points, and they wanted to see how we practised.

Naturally, after the party, we had the worst practice in the world. I stood at the side and let them fool around and have some fun.

So this coach put in the paper, "That was a disgrace. That is not the way to practise hockey. That's a disgrace to see the way Cherry lets them take it easy in practice," and everything like that.

So Harry is flyin' into town on Saturday with the Bruins' owner and they see the papers and I'm thinkin', "Boy oh boy, if we lose this game, Harry's not going to be happy."

So I didn't say nuthin' to the players. I just happened to leave a few papers lyin' around open to that page. I didn't have to say anythin' to the players. They knew. We were all under the gun.

I don't think Vancouver touched the puck! We played like it was the Stanley Cup championship game.

You never, ever give the other team any ammunition.

* * *

Sometimes, you get carried away as a coach. We played Washington and we beat them, but to keep the score down—and the referees used to do this, honestly—they'd give the winning team penalty after penalty after penalty.

They used to try to get the other team back in the game. We knew it. We didn't mind it. So I said after the game, "You know, I saw a horse race this afternoon. Instead of givin' us all those penalties, why don't they just put lead in our skates to make it even?"

Well, the Washington coach, Tommy McVie, went nuts. He wrote letters to the league that I should be fired. He wrote to Harry Sinden that I should be fired. We're going to play in Washington, and I get this long letter from him saying that I'm an awful guy, that I should be fired, that he's going to look into it. Et cetera, et cetera, as they say.

So just before we went out, I read his note aloud to the Bruins. I said, "Imagine this guy saying all this about us," and all that stuff. Well, of course, you couldn't hold them back. I think it was 6–0 in the first ten minutes. The Capitals weren't a very good team, so I'm not too proud of that. We could easily run up the score.

But I've got to tell you what I did to show you that sometimes as a coach, you get a little bit off balance in your head. As I walked by their bench—now get this—I stopped and read half of the letter to their players.

Their coach is standin' back of the bench and I'm readin' his letter on the ice and the referee is waitin' for the game to start.

I'll tell you, sometimes you get into that coachin' and you're mind goes a little kerphlooey.

As a little footnote, Washington was a team that never sold out. But after all that stuff hit the papers, you couldn't get a ticket.

* * *

I see Mike Milbury on television on TSN. I see him on NBC. I see him on the Bruins' TV broadcast. He has become Mr. Hockey on television in the States and now with CBC.

I wonder if he knows how close he came to not being involved in hockey, at least with the Boston Bruins.

In Rochester, when I was unemployed, I coached a high school hockey team. It was in Pittsford. Pittsford is a very rich little suburb on the outskirts of Rochester. They have a lot of money and I was unemployed, so I coached the high school. But I never got paid for it. Bob Clark, a lawyer and one-time part owner of the Rochester Americans, who was a good friend of mine who lived there, asked me if I'd coach the high school team, so I did.

While I was there, I had a young defenceman by the name of John Hoff, and he went on to play in the Ivy League at Colgate. He came back one summer, and I was coachin' Boston by then. He was tellin' me about playing at Colgate and said, "Boy, there's a guy there you should get a look at. He's a big, tough defenceman. He's not bad. His name is Mike Milbury."

Well, I forgot all about it.

The NHL teams always have a meeting in the summer and they go over who's comin' to training camp. We had about sixty guys comin', and for some reason, I said to the head scout, John Carlton, "John, isn't there a guy who plays around here, plays for a college like Colgate or Cornell or somethin'? Mulberry or somethin'?"

"Mulberry?" he says. "I don't know any Mulberrys. Oh, you mean Mike Milbury! Yeah, he's not bad."

"Okay," says I, "put him down. Add him to the end of the list. We'll give him a chance anyhow."

So he was about the sixty-first. That's how close he came to not comin' to the Bruins.

* * *

But he came to camp and he was pretty good, but he was like most American defencemen back in those days—he couldn't turn into the corners. Backin' up, he couldn't turn into the corners.

So I'll tell you what a dedicated guy he was. He had not a bad camp, but I tell him he's got to learn how to turn into corners if he's gonna make it to the NHL. So he goes to play back at Colgate, and next summer, he comes to my hockey camp in Rochester. He was one of the instructors.

So I get there early one morning, about 6:30. There's still fog on the ice. And here was his wife, Debbie, six months pregnant, on skates, dumpin' the puck in the corner. He was backin' up, turnin' in the corner. He did that for about an hour before the hockey camp started.

So he comes to the Bruins' camp that fall, and he is dynamite. He was the second-best defenceman at our camp—and you know who the first one was.

He looked so good and everythin' but I didn't tell him, but I sort of hinted that it looked like he'd made the team.

Well, I sit down with Harry Sinden to talk about who made the club, and right away, he says, "Milbury goes to Rochester."

I says, "What? Are you nuts? Harry, he's our second-best defenceman."

"No. He goes."

It was the first time and the only time Harry ever made a roster decision like that so that he could keep a first-round draft choice.

He kept a defenceman who was our first-round draft pick. The guy couldn't carry Milbury's jock, but Harry kept him.

So down goes Milbury to Rochester, heartbroken.

* * *

The season gets rolling and we were going along, doing good. There was a veteran defenceman on the club. I'm not going to mention his name, but everybody else bought into the system except him.

The system was that when the defencemen got the puck — except for Park, because Park was an All-Star — they put the puck around the boards and the wingers would be up there, and it would be out.

Well, this guy, he was older. He thought he was smarter than me and he was screwing everything up.

So I kinda made it hard for him for a month on. And another month on. And another month on. I'm givin' him a hard time. A coach can always do this.

And one day, he quits. He just quits! He walks up to Harry's office with twenty games to go in the season and quits.

I'll never forget how Harry told me. I was standing on the ice running the practice and I see Harry. In the Boston Garden, he had an office way up high, and he is comin' out of the office just steaming, coming down. And I know exactly what happened, 'cause the guy wasn't on the ice.

He comes over and he says, "What the **** is goin' on here? We got a veteran defenceman and twenty games left in the season, he wants to quit? What's goin' on?"

I says, "I don't know, Harry. I guess he just had enough."

So Harry says, "Well, we gotta bring Milbury up now."

So up comes Milbury and he plays a game in Buffalo, and he has turned into the softest guy you've ever seen in your life! I guess he got into the American league and decided he was gonna take it easy. I couldn't believe it.

On the bench, between every shift I'm calling him every name I can think of. There's lots of swearing and I'm calling him names. Commie. Softie. Left-wing pinko. College pacifist. I call him every name I can think of.

After the game, I take him aside and I get him up against the wall and I say, "Look, we're playin' our next game in Toronto and I don't care what's happening, the first guy that comes down the ice showin' any sign of looking for trouble, I want you to grab him and do what you have to do."

Sure enough, we're playin' in Toronto. He starts the game and the first guy that comes down, I think it was Pat Boutette, and Milbury does a number on him. And his career took off from there.

* * *

Let me tell you what happened the night before.

I go for a walk the night before the game in Toronto and I happen to drop into a bar. I go into this bar and there's Milbury! He's sittin' with a couple of our guys. Milbury! A rookie!

I gave it to those guys. I said to Milbury, "Get out of here, you son of a gun! The idea! Me gettin' you up here and you're out drinkin' the night before a game?"

Well, it wasn't really that bad. It was before midnight. But I had him wired pretty good.

And the next night, did he ever do his job! From then on, he was one of my most effective defencemen, I'll tell you that.

* * *

We eventually became the best of friends. He bought a house out in North Andover. It was a beautiful house out on Salem Drive. And it was a long drive in from North Andover and I lived there, so I picked him up.

He'd drive with me and we'd talk about hockey and what my ideas were and his ideas. I remember one day, I said, "I saw a great movie last night with John Wayne," and he said he didn't like John Wayne.

I said, "What? You don't like John Wayne? What kind of a guy are you? Who's your favourite actor?"

He says, "Woody Allen."

It figured.

* * *

One day we're drivin' in and we come to the Mystic River bridge and I looked and I saw a weed. The weed was growin' along the side, just sticking up at the side there, right alongside all of the traffic.

I said, "Mike? See that weed? That's what we gotta be like. That's what you gotta be like. Tough. See the rest of the weeds have all gone? That weed is still goin'."

Every time we'd drive in, I'd say, "Look at that weed, it's still there. See what I mean, Mike?"

Now, one day we're on the other side of the bridge, comin' back, and they're comin' along in the spring. They're gonna clean up all along the side. So I says, "Uh, oh. Look, Mike. It looks like they're gonna get our weed."

He says, "Oh no, they're not! Stop."

I pull over to the side. He dances among the traffic to the far side, got the weed and put it in the car.

He said, "They're not gonna get our weed."

They didn't. I kept it.

* * *

He had a great career. It lasted a long time and he coached.

When he was a player, he had a great attitude.

One time we were in Montreal—and you know how great the Canadiens were—and he was standing in the Forum, looking up at the pennants that they have across the top. They were made of wood, but they looked like pennants.

A French reporter came up to him and said, "Ah, Monsieur Milburee, I can see you're very impressed with our pennants."

He said, "To tell you the truth, I was lookin' at 'em and I was thinkin' they look rather chintzy."

* * *

Milbury was an American and he was a college guy and I understand he was the first guy to stand up to Alan Eagleson.

You must realize that in the eighties, Eagleson was the head of the players' union and he was a bully. If you said anything, or even asked a question he didn't like, he'd say, "Listen you dumb *******, you're a dum-dum. Just shut up."

I understand that Milbury was the first guy to stand up and say, "Hey, don't call me a dum-dum or ******* or I'll come up there and put your head through the wall."

That was the first time that the players saw that a player could stand up and do that to Eagleson. Milbury was an American. He didn't quite have the reverence we Canadians had for Eagleson. He was a college guy and I guess that had something to do with it.

But he was the first guy to put a little crack in Eagleson's power and eventually, as you know, Eagleson crumbled altogether and went to jail.

* * *

Gerry Cheevers, when he was in Boston, was quite a horse guy. He really played the horses. He knew horses. And he bought horses.

He had a beautiful horse called Royal Ski. At the time, it was neck and neck with Seattle Slew for which one was going to get named the horse of the year.

He sold Royal Ski to some Japanese guys and unfortunately, right after he sold him, the horse caught a virus and he had to give the money back.

That was his best horse.

I used to have a saying all the time, "Around the boards." I'd say, "When you get the puck, put it around the boards. Around the boards."

He used to hear that so much, he named one of his horses Around the Boards. It did pretty good, too.

* * *

Boston was a real place for the races—Rockingham Raceway and all that—but let's say some funny things happened there.

I knew these guys, they were holding this horse back. They would not let him win, but they knew it was a dynamite horse and they were holding him back.

So finally, the big day came when they were going to let him win.

Well, they didn't want to make a lot of bets around Boston, so what they did was they sent a guy out to Las Vegas to let him make bets out there.

So the next day, the guy who had sent the guy to Vegas comes in and he says, "I got good news and I got bad news."

So they said, "What's the good news?"

He says, "The good news is that the horse won and we had lots of money on him."

So they said, "Well, what can be the bad news?"

"Well, the guy that cashed the tickets stayed in the MGM Hotel. It had a fire and half of it burned down. He's dead and all the money's gone!"

* * *

My daughter Cindy was a walker for Gerry, and because she knew the horses pretty good, she told me this story.

Some guys she knew were holdin' back this horse named Timothy. He was a real good horse and he was always wanting his head to go, but they were waiting because the odds weren't right—or whatever they do.

So Saturday was goin' to be the day they were goin' to let him finally win one. The odds on the early line were good. Cindy said to the groom, "Big day Saturday for Timothy to win."

The groom said, "He won't win, Cindy. They have held him back for so long when he wanted his head to win that he'll end up second. He doesn't know how to win." And he didn't.

Some hockey players can be like that too.

* * *

I picked up the paper one day and I read, "Dennis O'Brien, a failure with his third team in one year."

I went to Harry that day and said, "I want Dennis O'Brien."

"Dennis O'Brien can't make Minnesota. We're a first-place club. And you want me to pick up Dennis O'Brien?"

I saw somethin' in him. I knew he wasn't a good skater, but I knew he would do as he was told. He was a defenceman, and the only defenceman I wanted handling the puck was Brad Park. The rest of them, I wanted it off the glass and around the boards.

I says, "Harry, do I ask for that much? What's it goin' to cost?"

He says, "Well, nothin'."

I says, "Well then, get him for me. If we get injuries, I can do somethin' with him."

He says, "Well, I don't understand it. It's absolutely ridiculous, a first-place club asking for a guy that can't make Minnesota. This will be his fourth club this season! He'll set a record for most teams in one year!"

Anyway, Harry got him for me. He came and he met us in Philadelphia and he was overweight. To say he was pudgy was bein' really kind.

He said, "What do you want from me? What's the word?"

I says, "I tell you what, Dennis. Meet me in the hotel bar tonight at nine o'clock."

So we're sitting there and we had a couple of pops and I got to know him. When you bring a guy in and you bring him into your office, it's like bringin' a kid into the principal's office. He's not goin' to tell you nothin'.

If you sit there and have a couple of beers, you kinda get an idea. It's not like you're getting drunk or anythin', but you sit there and he kinda loosens up a little.

So I found out what a couple of his problems had been and all that and he said, "What's our standard of play?"

I said, "Hand me that paper napkin," and I drew a diagram of the net and our end. I says, "See, this is our net. This is you with the puck. You put the puck off the glass. If you're not on with Park, it's off the glass or around the boards.

"If you're on with Park, you can give hit to him. Any other time, it's off the glass and around the boards."

I worked on him. I worked with him. I worked hard with him.

The Bruins used to have a lot of fun after practice because they were in dynamite shape, so I didn't really have to grind 'em. He's out there foolin' around with them too, and I called him over.

I said, "Dennis, you don't do what the rest of the players do."

He says "What do you mean?"

I said, "You're not goin' to have fun for a long time."

I worked him 'til he was almost dyin'. He became a thin hockey player. That's hard to believe—Dennis O'Brien, thin.

* * *

John McCauley told me the story.

Sometimes there is a time—and I've only seen it twice in my entire career—where by accident, everybody leaves the ice when they change on the fly.

What happened was, everybody left the ice except Dennis O'Brien. He was the only guy on the ice, and he's behind the net with the puck. There's nobody on the ice except him, the linesmen and the referee, John McCauley, who's standing at the blue line.

Dennis rings it off the glass and almost hits McCauley in the head.

McCauley goes back to him and says, "Are you out of your mind? There's no one on the ice. Why are you firing it off the glass like that?"

You know what Dennis said? "Grapes wants it off the glass? Grapes gets it off the glass."

He was a terrific player for us and one of my favourites.

* * *

We go into LA and in those days, everybody knew Gloria Loring. She was married to Alan Thicke.

She sang the anthems before the games, but she would not sing until the crowd went nuts. She'd stand there while they got all worked up. They loved her. She was worth a goal, she really was.

I just happened to say to Frosty Forristal, one of our trainers, "Gee, she gets them all worked up. She's worth a goal."

He says, "She really is? Would you like her not to be able to sing at centre ice?"

I says, "Yeah." I didn't know what he was talkin' about.

In those days, you had to have a cord for the microphone. They didn't have the cordless ones like they do now.

So she gets to centre ice and the crowd is all worked up and she lifts the mike and starts to sing, and there's silence!

Now the crowd dies down and one of the workers come out. But he can't fix it and she has to go over and sit in the penalty box and sing using the announcer's mike.

It ruined their whole thing.

Frosty had crawled underneath the seats and cut the wire!

We won the game.

AL'S NOTE: *A few years later, when the Edmonton Oilers were taking on the Kings in a playoff game in the same building, Don was working for* Hockey Night in Canada *and told this story to Oilers coach Glen Sather.*

Oddly enough, before the game the next night, the cord got cut again. Sather denied any involvement.

* * *

I was playing for the Sudbury Wolves of the Eastern Professional league and we played Kingston and we got beat out of the playoffs, so I come back home and the Kingston Frontenacs were going to play the Hull-Ottawa Canadiens.

Hull-Ottawa were a terrific team. Eleven guys went to the National Hockey League from there. So the game went on; I was in the crowd watchin'. Kingston were playing dynamite and this was for the championship game.

It was a wild game for a couple of reasons. It was the first time I'd ever seen a player get chased all over the ice, around and around. Terry Gray was in a fight, and there was a big schmozzle and he come out of it and started chasing this guy around and around. I'd never seen anythin' like it.

Anyway, the Frontenacs were up 2–0 in the third period—for the championship—and Harry Sinden and Barclay Plager fell in the corner.

So they're both in the penalty box and a player by the name of Tom "The Bomb" McCarthy—boy was he tough! He was a beautiful player. He could score goals. He had fifty goals in the Central league and never, ever got a shot in the National league.

He was so tough when we'd play against him—Darryl Sly and I—that Darryl would say, "Do you know who's on?"

He wasn't a goon. He didn't fight, but could he hit! And could he use that stick!

So Tom went over and asked Harry, "Harry, what happened?"

And Harry said, "Barclay kicked me when I was down."

And for some reason—to this day I'll never understand it—Tom the Bomb took his stick and hit Barclay right over the head and creased him like you couldn't believe.

Naturally, he got a five-minute major, and while he was in the box, Hull-Ottawa come on and won the game 3–2. It was unbelievable that a guy would do that—that a guy would do that and lose the hockey game.

I was watchin' it, but I couldn't believe it. He hit him right over the head! Five-minute major and they lost the championship.

Barclay was never the same after that. In fact, Barclay died of a brain tumour and his brother Bob, another tough guy who also played with the St. Louis Blues, told me that after Tom the Bomb hit Barclay over the head with that stick, he was never the same.

So everybody lost in that one. That was the most vicious thing I saw in a long time. It was a tough one to see.

* * *

The first time I met Harry Sinden, I was playing against him. He was playing for the Kingston Frontenacs.

He was from Whitby, and he had already played for the Whitby Dunlops overseas in the world championship tournament and had won the gold medal. He was a shifty defenceman, a smooth defenceman, and a lot of people don't know that he held the record for assists in professional hockey while playing for the Kingston Frontenacs.

And the guy who broke that record? Bobby Orr!

Harry was sort of like Brian Campbell in today's hockey, only smarter.

He became coach of the Oklahoma City Blazers. I was playing for Tulsa out there. It was tough playing against his teams. They were always aggressive and they would bang you pretty good.

Well, he graduated to the Boston Bruins, won two Stanley Cups as a general manager and as a coach. He come along at the right time—when Bobby come along.

He told me a story about being behind the bench when they were really struggling. A guy hollered, "Hey Sinden, there's a bus leaving for Oklahoma City in the morning. Be under it!"

And another guy hollered, "Hey Sinden, we named a city after you. Marblehead!"

They were tough in Boston, but he won the Cups, and as you know, he was the coach when Canada beat the Russians in '72, the greatest series maybe of all time.

AL'S NOTE: *The Whitby Dunlops were a Senior A team in an era when senior hockey held a prominent place in the hockey world. They won the world championship in Oslo, Norway, in 1958.*

* * *

My time in Boston was pretty good. Except for Milt Schmidt, I was the longest-running coach in Bruins history. There were a lot of victories and not too many defeats and there seemed to be turmoil the entire time.

It started out good. Harry and I were the best of friends. One time we were both going to the game—he was coaching Oklahoma and I was playing for Tulsa—and I was walking along and I could see him in the distance. I knew it was Harry because he had a big head. So we met as we were goin' to the door. Harry says, "Don, I knew it was you."

"How come?" I asked.

"Because of your cocky walk."

I said, "I knew it was you, Harry."

"How come?"

"Because of your big head."

* * *

So I knew Harry pretty good and I was doing pretty good in Rochester at the time. We had won the regular season. I was coach of the year, and when we were in the playoffs, I got a call from the Washington Capitals. They were going to come into the National Hockey League in the fall and they were asking if I wanted to coach there.

I said, "No, thanks." They were going to be an expansion team, and in that first year, they won eight games. So I turned that down.

Some time later, in June, I went to Montreal for the NHL draft. I was the coach and general manager in Rochester. I met Harry and the assistant GM, Tom Johnson, and while we were having breakfast, Harry asked me if I'd like to coach the Bruins.

And for some reason I've never ever been able to figure out, even though I had a pretty good thing goin' in Rochester—I was making $25,000, I had my own cars and was my own boss—I turned him down, if you can believe it.

And that night, I was sittin' there by myself havin' a pop by myself and I thought, "What a chicken!"

So I phoned Harry and met him the next morning for breakfast again and said, "I've changed my mind. I would like to coach the Bruins."

He said, "Don't you want to know for how much?"

I said, "Nope. Just give me a chance."

I got three years. At $40,000 a year.

* * *

So I go to the Bruins' training camp, and that was the time I went to a golf course and I couldn't believe the party that was goin' on. Girls walkin' around handing out cocktails! Guys half-smashed! And it was the night before training camp! Unbelievable.

I soon ended that when I got in charge.

Well, we got 94 points that year—the only time while I was there we got under 100—but like I said, in the first round, we got beat out by Chicago.

I am brokenhearted like you can't believe, and Harry is brokenhearted, so we have a meeting.

I said, "Look, Harry, I know I've got two years left, but for bein' beat out in the first round, you can say 'See you later' if you want."

He said, "No. I just want you to coach like you did in Rochester."

I knew what he was talkin' about. I was too soft on the players. They just kept sayin' to me, "Wait 'til the bell rings. Wait 'til the bell rings."

Well, the bell rang and we went out with two losses in three games.

* * *

After that, I wanted to have the toughest team in the league — which we did. We had four straight years of Adams Division titles. We had a winning percentage of .658. We made the finals twice, the semifinals twice, too. But unfortunately for us, we ran into some of the greatest teams of all time, the seventies Canadiens.

In fact, the '76 Canadiens were picked by *The Hockey News* as the greatest team of all time. My luck.

I'll just give you the starting lineup if you don't think it's true: left wing, Steve Shutt, 60 goals; centre, Jacques Lemaire, 34 goals; right wing, Guy Lafleur, 56 goals. On defence you had Larry Robinson. Say no more — Larry Robinson. Then Serge Savard, and if you want to put in Guy Lapointe, all three Hall of Famers. And if you get by them, you got Ken Dryden in goal, another Hall of Famer.

There was eleven Hall of Famers on that team. They were tough to beat, boy. One year, they only lost eight games all year, and only one at home. We were the team that beat them at home that one game, and we beat them three times that year. We beat them more than they beat us.

But the problem was when you get into a seven-game series with them, they had such depth that they'd finally get to ya. That's what happened with us.

Anyway, they won the Cups and I remember their coach Scotty Bowman saying to me that he and his wife were going to have a baby boy and they were going to name him Stanley.

And I says, "Well, when I have my baby boy, I'm gonna name him Finals."

* * *

I got the best draft story. This was in Boston in 1975. We're drafting and all the reporters down there tell me, "Listen, you've gotta get a guy that's playing quarterback. He's a hockey player. He plays quarterback for Vermont or New Hampshire, one of those places."

So I go to Harry and I says, "Harry," I says, "everybody tells me you gotta get this guy, this defencemen, a big defenceman. He's American. He's this; he's that."

Harry says, "Nah, we're not gettin' him."

We got Ronnie Grahame. We got Gilles Gilbert. We got Gerry Cheevers. They're all goalies. In the first round, they draft Dwight Foster. That was fine.

Then in the second round, they've got the thirty-fourth pick and they draft a goaltender called Davie Parro. He's about this big. (AL'S NOTE: *The height of Don's coffee table.*) So now we got four goalies. You know who the guy was that we coulda picked?

Rod Langway! You know who picked right after us with No. 36? Canadiens! They got him. We coulda had Rod Langway. He won the Norris Trophy. He was a first-team All-Star twice. He talked with a Boston accent. We coulda had the whole thing. We take Dave Parro! He was a nice kid, don't get me wrong, but Langway woulda loved it in Boston. We coulda had him. Imagine him and Brad Park! It would have been magic.

* * *

This is another one of those stories about moments to live forever.

I leave the New York Rangers camp and I'm going to be playing for the Kitchener Beavers in the Eastern Professional league.

What you must know is that after training camp, everybody gets a list of the apartments, and the way it works is you go with a buddy and you go down the list.

What happens is he gets the first one, then you get the second one, then he gets the third one, and so on. That's the way it works. You've got to stick to that all the time because if you don't, it's trouble.

Somehow or other, I got started late and I couldn't find one and I was goin' lookin' for apartments with this one guy—and he's sort of a selfish guy, eh? Everything was for him, him, him.

Then I looked for one and I didn't like it. Then he looked for one and he didn't like it.

So we're goin' on and we get to this apartment which should be my turn, and it's pretty good. It's up on the third floor, but it's really nice. It's got lots of room and it's open and everything, so I kinda look like I'm gonna take it.

Then I can see the guy talkin' to the landlord and he says, "So, you're Polish, eh? You know, my wife's Polish."

And they're talkin' back and forth. "Oh yeah, she makes Polish food," and so on, and I can see they were gettin' along great and now he wants the apartment. He says, "It would be nice for my wife."

And the landlord says, "Yes, I want him to have it."

Well, what am I gonna do? I gotta let him have it, even though it's not his turn, but I'm not too happy.

I get a call that night from Rose. She was in Hershey. "Well, have you found an apartment yet?"

"Er, no, not yet, Rose."

"Has the rest of the guys found apartments?"

"Er, yeah, they have, Rose."

"Hmmm." It was kind of frosty after that.

* * *

So the next day, the list is just about done. There's nothin' left, so I happen to go down to the hockey office after practice and I go in

Taking a slug after a Calder Cup win with Rochester. We won three Calder Cups and a final in four years.

Darryl Sly (my roommate and defense partner for six years), me, Duane Rupp, and Al Arbour.

(top) Cagey Mentor: That's Dennis O'Brien with the blond hair; he set a record of being with four teams in one year. We were his fourth and he played terrifically for us.

From *Sports Illustrated*.

Me in Russian hat. Carol Vadnais peeking over my shoulder. Bobby (MVP of the tournament). Scotty Bowman, coach of the 1976 Canada Cup team.

Blue and Rose in Boston. See story on p. 118.

My one and only Blue.

Rose in Boston. This is my favourite picture of her.

Timothy, Cindy, me, Del.

Me and Tim at the Christmas skate they
have every year in the Boston Garden.

Blue giving Harry Sinden the eye. Blue had run around the corridors at Boston Garden to get in the picture.
FRONT: Gilles Gilbert, Tom Johnson, Paul Mooney, Capt. Wayne Cashman, Me and Blue, Harry Sinden, Gerry Cheevers
MIDDLE: Dan Canny, Dick Redmond, Rick Smith, Jean Ratelle, Mike Milbury, Peter McNab, Terry O'Reilly, John Wensink, Al Secord, Donnie Marcotte, Frosty Forristal.
BACK: Jimmy B., Bobby Schmautz, Rick Middleton, Bobby Miller, Al Sims, Dennis O'Brien, Brad Park, Gary Doak, Stan Jonathan, Little Louie.

(left) The perfect gentleman, Danny Gallivan, the one word for Danny is elegant. I can still see him now with his cigarette holder studying the players in the warm-up at The Forum half an hour before the game. I never dreamed I would meet him, let alone broadcast colour with him.

(right) Ron in a top hat. See story on p. 146.

Brian Williams: The velvet voice. Our disagreement on the conduct of Canada's young junior players on the bench clearing brawl with the Russians was a beauty; our radio show on THE FAN 590 in T.O. has been going for 23 years.

　　Me, our bartender Jimmy Loftus, Ben Johnson, and Don Edwards, an NHL goalie who could really stone the Russians with his stand-up style. Tommy Knight, floor director, in the background.

Cam Neely, the ultimate power forward for the Bruins.

Me and Tie Domi, who never ducked a fight or picked his spots.

When a lady saw this picture she said, "that is the handsomest man I have ever seen." Of course I thanked her and said, "Kirk's not bad looking too!"

Dougie Gilmour, is he good looking or what? That goal he scored against Curtis Joseph in the '93 playoffs was one of the greatest goals I've ever seen. A little guy with a huge heart who should be in the Hall of Fame.

Eric Lindros, me with glasses on because I am covered in poison ivy, and Kirk Muller at the Grapevine.

Two team mates from Eddie Shore's Springfield Indians: Brian Kilrea, winningest Junior coach of all time with the Ottawa 67's, we had many adventures together; and Dennis Olsen, no matter the situation Dennis always had a smart quip.

Kenny Reardon, hard-rock defenseman for the Montreal Canadiens. In the Second World War he was awarded a medal for bravery. Guy Lafleur, after Bobby I liked to watch him play. I can see him now, flying down the ice with hair flowing behind him. The Flower took a lot of abuse but I never saw him complain. He had style and class. And my buddy Dick Irvin, he and Danny Gallivan were the best combo ever in sports.

to see the secretary there and I says, "Is there any more apartments I could look at?"

And she says, "Yeah, this here one just come in."

So I says, "Well, I'll give it a try." I go over and it's unbelievable. It's a house! It's a beautiful, brand new house! It was gorgeous, best one we ever lived in, I think, in all of my hockey career.

In the basement, I think, were two nurses, and we were up above. We had a back yard for Cindy to play in. It was like you had a brand new house, so we lucked out on that one.

Rose always said that of all the places we travelled, she liked Kitchener the best. It was the cleanest, and the apartment we lived in was the best. We were used to livin' in some strange places that were awful.

Now, this same guy I went apartment-hunting with, about two months later, comes into the house with his wife to visit us.

They were sitting there and his wife looks around and says, "Oh my! what a beautiful spot. I just love it.

"And Don, it's so considerate of you. Not like him. He's got me on the third floor. Gotta lug up all the groceries all the time."

Oh, he was so mad! He took off.

He had a beautiful DeSoto, a beauty car. He walked out and sat in the car, just sitting there fuming until she got ready to leave.

Oh boy. Moments to live forever.

* * *

When I played for the Kitchener Beavers, I was in the other team's corner with a guy—I don't know what I was doin' *there*—and for some reason, I was in a fight with this guy. He was a big guy, about six foot three. So we dropped the gloves and we started throwin' 'em, and he could not fight at all.

But he was big. He reminded me of Dale Rolfe. Remember the number Dave Shultz did on him and he wouldn't stop? So this was almost the same thing. But I stopped because he couldn't defend himself the way he should. It was Terry Harper, and he went on to play for the Montreal Canadiens.

Then a strange thing happened. There was a guy on our bench—I'm not gonna mention his name, but he was an older guy like me, and Terry Harper was just startin' out. He saw that Harper couldn't fight, and later in the game, he jumped him.

All the players on the bench knew what he was doin'. He saw Harper couldn't fight and now he's gonna fight him. Nobody respects a guy who does that.

Terry got more experienced, and by the time he got to the National Hockey League, he could throw 'em pretty good. But anybody worth his salt will never beat up on a kid that can't fight.

* * *

The strangest thing happened in that game.

Again, I'm in the other team's end. I don't know why, but that was the year I got thirteen goals. I was in a head-to-head contest with this other defenceman that had jumped Harper. The other guys disliked this guy so much that they knew that him and I had this point thing goin', and they'd give me their assists so I'd beat him.

You could see Terry Harper was goin' to the National Hockey League. He was a tryer. He had knocked down one of our players and was sittin' on him at centre ice. I don't know what I was doin' backcheckin', but I was backcheckin' and I knocked Harper off and I sat on him.

I had him down. I wasn't gonna hit him, but I let on I was gonna hit him. I had my arm cocked and it was right in front of their bench, maybe about twenty feet in front of their bench.

And not one of their players came on the ice to help him! I'm sittin' there lookin' at them, waiting for one of their tough guys to come on and they all just sat there!

You know who was gonna come on? Floyd "Busher" Curry. And

he was the coach! Remember Busher Curry? He was comin' over the boards to get me and the guys had to hold him back.

What a great guy he was.

* * *

In the *Boston Globe* there was a great big front-page picture in the sports section and it had a picture of the Boston Bruins with Blue sitting on my lap. Harry was not too happy. It said, "Bruins go to the dogs."

What happened was we were getting our team picture taken in front of the visiting team's bench and the Zamboni door was behind us. I had Blue down there and Frosty Forristal, the trainer, put a goalie mask on Blue and Blue was barking.

I shouted, "Come on, Blue. Come and get your picture taken." Well, naturally, she didn't come across the ice and all the guys are saying, "Hah, she's not too smart."

Well, as God is my judge, she ran all the way around the Boston Garden, come up through the stairs and was right in front of us at the visiting bench. She knew enough not to go on the ice. The guys couldn't believe it.

I'll never forget the very first time Wayne Cashman saw her. She was in the dressing room and Cash thought he was going to be smart. He put the stick down to her and was kind of going to tease her. She grabbed his blade and snapped it in two.

That was the last time anybody ever teased Blue.

Gosh, I loved Blue, and I do miss her.

* * *

Blue and I had a favourite song. It was by Stevie Wonder and it was called "You Are the Sunshine of My Life."

Well, one day, about a year after Blue died, Rose and I are driving along somewhere and that song came on the radio. I got so upset, I thought I was having a heart attack. When we arrived at the hotel, I had to sit in the lobby to calm down. I still get misty when I hear that song twenty-five years later.

In fact, I'm getting misty now.

* * *

I'm in the EPHL with the Three Rivers Lions, if you can believe it.

It's a beautiful spot to play and the people were great. I had a grand time there. A lot of snow.

Cindy was about three at the time and she'd walk around in there in a little blue playsuit. It was a really old building, though. Fans were really rabid and great.

If you made a real good goal or made a real good play, believe it or not, they'd pass two-dollar bills down to the trainer to give to ya.

I never won the $2 ever, but I used to see the other guys get it.

One of the guys on the club was really cheap. One day, Rose was waitin' outside after the game as the wives do, and she looked down and found a $10 bill. This guy started on his wife: "Why can't you ever do anything like that?".

* * *

Nobody spoke English, but we still had a grand time. There was no English television except for starting at eleven o'clock at night once a week, when there'd be an hour and a half of English television, and it was always one of those old horror movies—Bela Lugosi and all that.

So we used to get in Chinese food and be all happy that we were gonna see one hour and a half of English television.

Sometimes, the bus would sit outside our window and idle, and when it did that, because the TVs had rabbit ears for an antenna in those days, it would interfere with the television and we'd be all ticked off.

One time, Rose went into the beauty shop and she couldn't speak French and they couldn't speak English. So she held her fingers a couple of inches apart and said, "I just want about this much off."

Well, at this time, all the French girls had short haircuts, so they thought Rose was showin' how long she wanted it, and they gave Rose a brush cut. I come home and she was in tears because she had long, beautiful black hair.

I gotta admit, though, she looked pretty good.

* * *

We played one time on a Sunday afternoon—this was with the Three Rivers Lions—and after the game, there was a party at my house.

It was unbelievable this apartment we had. We had a great big kitchen. The kitchen was about fifty feet by fifty feet and the bedroom—and it only had one bedroom—had to be about ten by ten.

Cindy had to sleep on the floor on a single mattress, but the kitchen for some reason was enormous. In the centre was a table. It was round and it had to be ten feet across. The apartment had a nice bathroom, and it was cold, but we survived.

After the game, I said, "Everybody have a party back at my house," and boy, they could drink back in those days.

All the wives came and they were sittin' in this little wee living room and all the guys were out in this big kitchen, drinkin' as usual.

Two of the referees showed up and they came in with two French girls. The guys knew the referees were married, and it got kind of frosty in there.

But while we're in there, we get drinkin' and it gets to be two in the morning. It had been snowing, and by the time we go outside, there has to be four feet of snow. Guys can't find their cars. It was like in a movie.

One of the guys tripped. He was three-quarters stiff and he fell down in the deep snow and he's buried in the snow. We look up and the snowplow is comin'.

If I hadn't have gone out and dragged him and pulled him back, he'd have gone right under the snowplow.

* * *

The next morning, I wake up and I have to get up and go to practice. I look in the kitchen and there has to be at least a hundred beer bottles sittin' there on top of that big table.

I had to go to practice, so I didn't have time to put them away, so Rose was goin' to have to do it.

But Rose was pretty understanding. I don't know how she put up with me.

As everybody used to say, "Rose, there'll be a medal in heaven when you get there for puttin' up with this guy."

* * *

When we were on the buses and we'd go from Quebec into Ontario, we'd always pick up Red Cap beer.

In Ontario, back when I was startin' to drink at the age of twenty-one, every tavern had Carling's Red Cap Ale on draft. They had other ones later, but all the hockey players drank Red Cap.

You never could get Carling Red Cap Ale in Quebec—naturally, because the red cap on the label is an English cap and all that. If you looked at the back of the bus when we'd been in Ontario and we were going back to Quebec, it would be all piled up with Red Cap beer.

We had our priorities in the minors.

* * *

Like I said, Harry hired me for the Bruins and stuck with me after we went out in the first round.

So we had a meeting before the next season and he says, "Look Don, we gotta win. Do whatever you gotta do. Make me the heavy.

Make anybody the heavy, because if you don't win, we're both gone."

So unfortunately, I took it to the extreme. I took the Bruins and had them thinkin' the world was against them. I made Harry the number one enemy, which was wrong, but like he said, we had to win.

I worked at it. We were a first-place club and it was near the end of the season and in Chicago, the NHL had a list of favourites who were gonna win the Cup and they didn't even mention us.

I went on a tirade with all the sportswriters. I remember one guy was sitting there asking me questions and I just had a feeling he wasn't a sportswriter.

I said, "Who are you? Who are you? Get out! Get out, you ****," and they got it on tape and played it on one of those underground tapes.

Anyhow, I had everybody thinking it was us against the world. I told one writer, "You know, with the Bruins, it's like if there were tribes of Indians and all the tribes were in a valley with their fires going. And all the different NHL tribes were there. And there would be the Bruins, up on a cliff, with *their* fire goin'."

We were the favourites in Boston. We were more popular than the Red Sox, the Celtics and the Patriots, so we were doing something right.

* * *

One of the reasons that we were so popular was that a lot of people don't realize Boston is a lunch-pail town.

In the south of Boston, they have the Southies, as they call them. They're the Irish. And in the north, they have the Italians, hard workers.

Fran Rosa, a writer there for the *Boston Globe*—and I know they've used it in other places since, but we were the first—called us the Lunch Pail Gang. They punched in at 7:30 and they never stopped workin' until ten o'clock.

I played on a lot of hockey clubs that were hard workers, but nobody ever worked as hard as these guys. I tell ya, they were really somethin' to watch.

We went into Buffalo and one of the writers there, I think it was Dick Johnson, said, "The Bruins play as if they are in a frenzy."

And one of the Buffalo players said, "If we woulda worked as hard as the Bruins, we would have won."

We were tough and we could score. We scored over 300 goals.

Harry came into my office one time, sat down and says, "You know what? We scored 300 goals again. How did we do it?"

I said, "I don't know."

If I did, I'd probably screw it up.

AL'S NOTE: *The Bruins scored more than 300 goals in every year of Don's tenure. In the 1974–75 season, they scored 345. By comparison, the 2006– 07 Bruins scored 219. The 2007–08 Bruins scored 212.*

* * *

For the first four years, Harry and I were the closest friends. We used to go over and eat Chinese food at his house. He could make Chinese food. It was his specialty.

He used to take all day to make Chinese food and he'd eat it in about two minutes.

He was the fastest eater I've ever seen.

I was rollin' along. Everybody liked me. I won the Adams Trophy as coach of the year. I was voted coach of the year by the coaches. They had a poll. It was really somethin'. I couldn't do anything wrong.

One of the reasons was that if the sportswriters needed a column, they could call my house. Even if it was eleven o'clock at night, if they didn't have anything, they could phone. I'd be up watchin' Johnny Carson or something and I'd do a column for them.

So they'd protect me.

I remember after a tough loss, I used to go into a tirade about Mr. Campbell and Harry and referees and the league and everything.

And I'd wake in the morning and go, "Oh no! What have I done now?" and get the papers and there wouldn't be a word about it. They'd protect me. They were the best.

Don Zimmer, the Red Sox manager, told me one time, "I don't understand it. I win 93 games, set a record and they hate me. You're out in the first round and you're a hero."

* * *

One of the reasons was that I looked like a Southie to the gallery gods. I was big. I was heavy. And by accident, I wore a green cap like they wear, and it had a little tassel on top. I wore it all the time so I looked more like a Southie than a Southie.

In Boston, it goes by what you wear and look like.

But things started to happen. We started to win—eighteen straight, first place—and I started to think I was doin' it myself.

After one game, I said, "You know, Harry, I felt like I was Admiral Nelson out there. I was in command and we won the game."

He looked at me. I was gettin' carried away with myself.

We were first place four straight times. Everything was goin' great and unfortunately, I started thinking *I* was doin' it.

You can't start thinkin' that way. You might be able to guide the players a little, but they're the ones that are doin' it.

* * *

A little footnote here.

When I went to work on *Hockey Night in Canada*, the president of the Bruins phoned Ralph Mellanby, the executive producer.

He said, "You'd better be careful of Cherry. When he was with the Bruins, he thought he was Lord Nelson."

Ralph said, "Oh, we're okay. Now that he's working here, he thinks he's the head of the CBC."

* * *

As a coach, I never matched lines. I see coaches match lines, but I remember when I played, I played for a couple of coaches that matched lines.

I always felt it worked against the flow of the game. The guys were looking at the coach: Do I go? Do I not go? Do I stay on? Do I come off?

Guys would just get on for ten seconds, then off they'd come. They never seemed to get into the flow of the game.

When I was a coach, I knew who to match. As long as I knew who to match, that was enough. The team didn't need an explanation.

I always felt that when you tell your guys what a great team the other team is and say, "Watch this guy. Watch that guy," you weren't doing them any favours. If you did that with the Montreal Canadiens of the seventies, you'd be beat before you even got started.

You'd start off by saying, "Let's check their first line: Shutt with 60 goals; Lemaire with 34 goals; Lafleur with 56 goals."

Then you go to Robinson, Lapointe, Savard. You're saying how great they are. What's the sense of playin' them?

I always felt that sort of thing was negative. If we lost a game 4–1 but won two fights, on the video before the next game, I'd show our one goal and the two fights. That's the way I felt.

AL'S NOTE: *The Canadiens' line of Steve Shutt, Guy Lafleur and Jacques Lemaire terrified goalies in the 1976–77 season when they racked up the goal totals Don mentions. Shutt had 105 points, Lafleur had 136 and Lemaire, the "defensive specialist" on the line, had 75.*

* * *

If you talk to players, they really hate matchin' lines. What I'd do is put a checker on each line, so I could depend on every line.

One time I had Jean Ratelle, Bobby Schmautz and Donnie Marcotte on a line. Each of them had over twenty goals and each of them could check.

In Buffalo, the Sabres had the French Connection line, and every time I'd put on Jean Ratelle's line, they'd take off the French Connection line.

Any time I could get that line sitting on the bench, I'd be happy. I knew they were upset. They'd go by our bench and you could hear the cursing. They were really upset.

That's how we ended up with eleven guys who had twenty goals or more—because we played everybody all the time. We had a flow goin' all the time, a nice flow.

I feel sorry for these guys sometimes when I see them go on for six seconds, then jump off. That's no way to play.

You're going to say, "Well, didn't you check at all?"

I always had my ace in the hole, a guy called Donnie Marcotte. Every time their big line went out, no matter who went out, I'd just kind of sneak in Marcotte at the right time. He could make any line a checking line.

AL'S NOTE: *The French Connection line was Gilbert Perreault, Rene Robert and Richard Martin. It was one of the most prolific lines of the seventies, their most productive season being 1974–75 when every player on the line had at least 40 goals: Perreault had 44, Robert had 40 and Martin had 52. But the Buffalo Sabres never won a Stanley Cup. The French Connection took them as far as game six of the Stanley Cup final against Philadelphia in 1975.*

* * *

My Blue was an inspiration to me. She never looked for a fight and never ducked one.

Two people she really liked were Rene Robert from the French Connection line and my buddy Whitey Smith.

I don't know why, but they were her favourites. She loved to sleep with Whitey.

One day, Rene came to the house with some friends. Blue didn't greet anybody. If you wanted to see her, you came to her.

On this day for some reason—I guess to impress his friends—Rene called Blue and snapped his fingers for her to come.

Blue walked out and couldn't believe someone had snapped his fingers at her. She looked at me as if to say, "Can you believe this?" then turned and walked away.

Rene said, "Gee, Don, doesn't Blue like me any more?"

She never forgave him and never bothered with him again.

There is a picture of her and Rose in the book. Isn't it great? Blue is ready for anything.

* * *

One time we were flyin' back from Atlanta. Harry wouldn't get us a charter, so we had to get up at five in the morning and fly back, and we couldn't land in Boston because there was a snowstorm. We had to fly on to Hartford and land there.

I'm often asked, "What was the scariest plane trip you've ever taken?"

Well, there has been a lot. I told you the story about the one into Chicago when we circled in the plane over Lake Michigan trying to get into Chicago O'Hare.

But I think the very worst was this one.

I'll tell you, you couldn't believe the snowstorm. You couldn't see anythin'. We were bouncin' all over and we were sittin' at the back.

We really thought this was the biscuit. Some of the guys were really nervous. We thought we were gonna have it right there.

I said, "Well, guys, if we go down, we go down in first spot."

There was a pause, and then Milbury said from the back, "Yeah, and with a game in hand."

Everybody broke up at that one.

We finally landed in Hartford. We had to go and get cars, believe it or not. This is the National Hockey League and they didn't have a bus waitin' for us. We had to rent cars, take our equipment in the cars, get back and play the Canadiens, who had been in their beds while we were playin' in Atlanta. That story is comin' up.

* * *

I mentioned about havin' to fly in from Atlanta.

Well, Sammy Pollock, he was the smartest guy in hockey ever. What he did was, we were goin' for first spot and we had to win these games with Montreal.

Well, Montreal had a game scheduled for Saturday night with Washington, while we were playin' in Atlanta.

So Sammy talked to Washington and says, "Is it all right if we switch the game to the afternoon?"

Well, Washington didn't want to tick off Sammy Pollock. They agreed. So the Canadiens played the game in the afternoon, then flew to Boston. They're in their beds watchin' us play in Atlanta on Saturday night!

We had to get up at five in the morning, go through that flight with the snowstorm, have the guys try to have a little nap in the afternoon—in the dressing room, if you can believe it—and have the game that night.

We're winnin' 2–1, but they tie it up and it ends up as a 2–2 tie.

So I'm walkin' along the hall in the Garden back to my office, and Red Fisher, the dean of hockey writers at the time—he's from the *Montreal Star* and he's been there for 200 years—he's walkin' along with me.

I'm muttering, mostly to myself, "That son of a gun Harry, if he hadn't been so cheap, if he would have got us a charter, we would've won that game. The guys just ran out of gas."

So a little later, I'm sittin' in my office at my desk, with Harry across from me, and Red strolls in and says, "Hey Harry, Grapes says you woulda won that game if you hadn't been so cheap and had got a charter."

Harry turned and looked at me. He says, "Did you say that?"

I almost fell off the chair. I swallowed. I said, "Yeah."

Things were never the same between Harry and me, and I owe it all to Red Fisher.

And you know what Red Fisher says today?

"Hey, if I hadn't got you fired, you wouldn't be on television. You owe me a lot."

That Red, he's always got an answer.

* * *

So Harry and I really got into it the last year. It was sad to watch.

In the first round of the playoffs, we're getting ready to play Pittsburgh and we're having our morning skate.

Frosty Forristal, the trainer, come out and he said, "Harry has called a meeting. He wants everybody in the room."

I couldn't believe it. It was the first time he had ever done this. You could see how bitter it had become. That made it look like he was trying to make me look bad.

So he called everybody in the room and we looked up and he's got the lines written on the board, which I never did.

I never, ever had the Bruins work on lines. We never checked *them*. I always went positive. Let *them* check *us*.

I look and I see he's got a guy named Jim Hamilton on the right wing on the second line. I think, "Wait a minute. Jim

Hamilton is not even there. He scored a hat trick about a month before, and they kept him a week and sent him back down to the minors."

But Harry has got him up there and all the players look at me. I just put my finger to my lips: Don't say a word.

So Harry's going on, "We gotta check lines. We gotta do this. We gotta do that."

He come to Hamilton and he says, "We got to check that Hamilton."

So someone went to say something, but I just put my finger to my lips and said nothin'.

Well, right away, all his credibility was gone. He's talking about a player who hasn't been there in a month.

He finishes and storms out of the room, and the players put on the board, "Hamilton who?" and "Are you kiddin'?" and stuff like that on the board.

I shoulda rubbed it off, but unfortunately I didn't, and Harry heard it all, that the players were makin' fun of him.

The funny thing is that somebody wrote down, "Three straight. A piece of cake." And we did beat them three straight.

But it just went downhill from there—him sending me notes and staying in different hotels. It was really bad, and it was sad, too, because we had a good thing going.

The players hadn't got tired of me. They still loved me. I loved them. But I knew it was time to go.

* * *

The papers took my side, of course.

One cartoon was really good. It had me walkin' into Harry's office and Harry is sitting back at his desk. His right hand is hangin' down and he's got a great big revolver. And he says, "Come in, Don. I want to talk about your lifetime contract."

The best one was a cartoon in the *Boston Globe*, and it had Blue sniffing around Harry Sinden's office and Blue is saying, "Yeah,

Grapes. I'll be right there. I just want to leave a little something for Harry."

We went out losing to Montreal, the first-place club, and unfortunately, we had too many men on the ice. But we give it a good shot. Overtime in seven games. We were still havin' fun, and that's the way to leave. We left on a high note.

I loved the guys. They loved me. Hey, nothing goes on forever.

* * *

One of the very first interviews I did when I got back from Colorado and I was on television, I was on with Dick Beddoes.

He was a great sportswriter, I thought, from Hamilton, Ontario. He was a feisty guy and we were interviewing Harold Ballard, the owner of the Toronto Maple Leafs, so I was a little nervous.

You kind of feel your way when you first start on television. You don't have confidence. I don't care what anybody says, when the floor director goes, "Five, four, three," and then puts up two fingers, then one, then points at you, it's a bit scary. More on that a bit later.

So I was tryin' to do my best and I had a rose on. Naturally, it wasn't a real rose. It was a silk rose. And at the end of the interview, with the camera still on, Dick Beddoes said, "That rose is fake, isn't it?"

I didn't know what to say. Then he said, "I wonder what else about you is fake."

I was speechless.

But afterwards, I got on pretty good with him. I really liked him. He was just nailin' the rookie, I guess.

A couple of years later, we were on a call-in show, Dick Beddoes and I, and a caller asked, "Don, what do you do with your old clothes?"

Dick thought he was a dandy dresser and I said, "I just give them to Dick here. Can't you see?"

Gotcha!

* * *

When I started doing banquets, I was a little nervous, but I had to do them to survive. Molson's gave me $750 to do a banquet and I needed the money.

I had come from Colorado and I'd had to buy a house, and *Hockey Night in Canada* at the time, you were lucky to be on. It paid nothin'.

I was doing six banquets in five nights in five different cities.

One I did was in Calgary, and Bobby Hull had just flown in. Bobby, he was a good speaker, but not as good as his brother Dennis. Dennis is the best. But Bobby's good too, though he made the mistake of saying, "I just flew in from Belleville and it was sunny and I had a round of golf before I flew out."

Well, it was wet and miserable in Calgary and he's going on about Belleville.

This guy stood up and yelled, "Well, if you like Belleville so much, why don't you go back?"

It was a tough crowd. I got up after Bobby and I says, "I just left Toronto and it was rainy and miserable."

They liked that.

AL'S NOTE: *Dennis Hull is widely considered hockey's best after-dinner speaker, and most of his routine is based on making fun of Bobby. Arguably, his best line is this one: "Everybody thinks that Bobby wasn't that tough a player, but that's not true. Why, one year alone, he put three people in hospital. Of course, they were all in the maternity ward."*

* * *

The guy up before me was named Dave Cutler and he was a famous kicker in the Canadian Football League. But I'd been coachin' in Colorado, and before that I was in Boston. I didn't know who he was.

I was sittin' beside him and he proceeded to get up and he just roasted me. It was unbelievable.

I didn't mind. Everybody was laughin', so that was all right, but I didn't know what to say because I didn't know the guy. I really didn't know the guy.

So I get up there and I says, "So Dave—Dave is it?—I'd like to roast you back but I don't know who the **** you are!"

Well, it was one of those deals where they laughed so hard, that I'd start to speak and they started laughin' again.

I know a lot of guys use that line now, but it was honestly said and I kinda felt a little bad afterwards because I really did hurt him.

But it's the old story, as I've said many times, you play with the bull, you get the horn.

* * *

Some of the speakers at these banquets, they're really somethin'. One time, there was this guy and they couldn't get him off. He was from the States and he was talking about American college basketball.

They really, seriously, couldn't get him off. They had a guy who literally had to go up there and kind of push him off.

There was one guy who went on and on, and every time he paused, the crowd would clap. But he just kept goin' on.

Finally, everybody stood up on their chairs and waved their napkins. Even that didn't stop him.

Another one I saw one time, I think it was in Regina, the guy went on too long and he was kinda drinkin'. There was 2,000 people in the audience and they started bangin' their glasses to get him off.

Another time, the announcer got up and said, "Good news. So-and-so won't be back."

Evidently, he was the speaker the year before and he did a lousy job, and everybody cheered. When I got up to do mine, I said, "Wherever I am, next year at this time, when you have this banquet, I'm comin' back."

And they all cheered. I said, "You're not gonna talk about me that way."

Sometimes those banquets get awful vicious, I tell ya.

* * *

One time, for Green Cross fertilizer—and I know what you're thinking: fertilizer—we went across the Prairies in the middle of winter.

Drumheller! I didn't even know where I was, but I remember the name Drumheller.

We were goin' city to city, and like I said, I did six banquets in five nights. I did two in the one day.

We had stopped for lunch in some small town on our way to another banquet that night. While I'm sittin' there, this guy come over and said, "We're having a lunch meeting over at the Elks. You want to come over and speak?"

I did it. I needed the money.

That's how I did six in five nights.

* * *

You've heard about people who travel and wake up in the morning and have no idea where they are? That was me doin' banquets.

I remember sitting in the back of a church somewhere, listening to a church organ and having a little meal that was on my lap.

So this one time, we were out west, and I don't know what city. I really don't.

It was an "I'm really glad to be here" deal. And I'm tellin' jokes and I look out, and there's not even a smile.

I tell another joke and there's not even a smile again.

I can hear the guys that have brought me here laughin' in the back, so I figure, well, if you liked that one, here's another one.

Again, not a smile from the crowd. Not even a chuckle. They all got up and left.

The guys told me after, they were all Mormons.

Imagine, me up there talking about guys drinkin' and Wayne Cashman beatin' guys up and they're all Mormons!

I tell ya, it wasn't an easy life when I first come back from Colorado.

* * *

When I was at the Canada Cup training camp in 1976, I got to know Sammy Pollock a little—if anybody got to know him, because he was an awful quiet guy.

We were driving to a game or a practice on the bus.

I don't know where we were goin', but we had about an hour's drive and he was sittin' there across from me and they were talkin' about nights. Come to think of it, we were goin' to a night for somebody.

Sam was just sittin' there, lookin' out the window. That's great for conversation. Then he turned to me and said, "Did you ever have a night, Don?"

I thought for a minute, "Yeah, well, I had a night in Rochester."

He says, "Oh, you did? What happened?"

I started to think, "Well, let me see what I got."

Sammy is used to guys getting boats and cars and everything. I says, "Well, I know I got a bushel of apples. I know I got a golf shirt."

And he's looking at me to see if I'm serious and he's startin' to chuckle. But I am being serious.

"And I got a country club membership. The only thing was, the country club was 120 miles outside of Rochester. And I remember Max's Color Television Shop, he gave me a black-and-white television. And I got a dinner downtown."

Well, Sammy starts laughin', and when I say, "I was happy to get the golf shirt," he started to cough. You know one of those deals when you start coughin' and you start chokin'? Well, he got laughin' and nobody ever saw Sam laugh. If you know Sam, you know you never saw him laugh. Or smile.

And he was laughin' so hard, he started to choke. And one of the team doctors, I think it was Dr. Head, had to come back and treat him.

My night, I really appreciated it. My mom come down and my brother come down. It was at centre ice. But I guess the bushel of apples kinda set Sam off.

* * *

A lot of people wonder where I get those clips for "Coach's Corner."

I watch an awful lot of hockey games. I start at seven o'clock at night and I watch 'til 1:30 in the morning. It's my hobby and it's nice to be able to work at somethin' that's also your hobby.

I also go out to watch the minor midgets. My son, Tim, is an Ontario Hockey League central scout, so he rates all the kids in the Greater Toronto Area and we go out two or three times a week.

While I'm away, the genius behind "Coach's Corner" is a young girl called Kathy Broderick.

She's a little red-headed girl, and the first time she started at *Hockey Night in Canada,* they told her to go and get the stats.

Well, when we were over at Maple Leaf Gardens, it was awful, that studio we had. So she was getting the stats. She had just started, and she was talkin' while I was tryin' to talk.

There was only fifteen seconds left in the broadcast, so here she was gettin' the stats and we were goin' off the air.

I didn't want to be mean to her, but I says, "Hey, you over there. There's no sense gettin' the stats with ten seconds to go 'cause we're gonna be off the air. We don't need them, and don't talk while I'm tryin' to talk."

Well, she's a redhead, eh? And you know what they're like. A few minutes later, she comes marchin' up to me and she says, "Listen, Mr. Cherry, I was told to do a job and I'm gonna do it to the best of my ability."

And she turned around and walked away.

I thought, "Ooh, what a little firecracker she is!"

She told me later that she was scared skinny that she was gonna get fired.

She's the person now that gets me all my stats. I phone up now and I say, "Kathy, somethin' happened in the Dallas game."

And she says, "Yeah, this guy hit that guy." She knows exactly what I want. She finds things when I'm out. She says, "I think you'll like this one here. It shows so-and-so. I've got it for you."

She's the one. People never hear about her, but she's the one that does the job. Any time I wanna know anything that's goin' on, or anything that's happening, or where I'm supposed to go, all I have to do is phone Kathy Broderick.

I always think back to that little firecracker coming up and saying, "Listen, I'm gonna do my job."

I knew she was a beauty back then.

* * *

One day, I said to her, "Kathy, if they ever get rid of you, I'll leave the CBC."

She said, "Don't say that in public, Grapes. They'll get rid of me for sure."

She's sort of a wise guy.

* * *

Composite sticks. Listen, I know they make the shot go harder.

I know. I've watched Patrick O'Sullivan. He was with the Mississauga Ice Dogs. He was one of the first kids to get one when he was young. He could make the stick do tricks.

I saw him one time, he let his shot go and it was so hard it disappeared. That's one of the reasons we have so many foot injuries— these shots are so hard.

I would say Jason Spezza does pretty good shooting with a

wooden stick. And what about Al MacInnis? Did anybody ever have a harder shot than Al MacInnis?

He always used a wooden stick. I really do believe we should go back to the wooden sticks.

Take a look at baseball. Everybody knows that you can hit the ball farther with an aluminum bat, but they keep wooden bats. It's traditional.

Also, it would change the game. A good pitcher will break a bat with a pitch in on the hands. With an aluminum bat, that great pitch gets hit down the line for a double.

Everybody knows that if you use one of those new golf clubs with the squares in front, even a punk can hit the ball far. But they're not allowed in tournaments.

In other sports, they tell guys what they can't use.

You know one of the reasons that I really want to do it—one of the main reason other than injuries?

It's to help parents with kids in minor hockey. To see a single mother have to go out and spend $200 on a stick is heartbreaking. But if you're a mom, what are you going to do?

It's peer pressure. Say Jimmy's dad goes out and buys him a $300 composite stick. And Johnny comes home and says, "Jimmy's dad just bought him a $300 stick." What are you going to do? You have to go out and buy one.

I really believe hockey would be better without composite sticks. I see no reason for them.

You see guys go to take a shot and the stick breaks in two. Guys get penalties for just tapping them and they break in two. And besides that, you have a minor-league team and it's tough to make ends meet.

Neil Smith, the former Rangers GM, said on his club, the bill was $40,000 for sticks. Absolutely ridiculous!

We should go back to wooden sticks and hockey would be better.

Gretzky and Bobby Orr and Gordie Howe didn't do bad with wooden sticks.

AL'S NOTE: *Like Don, Gretzky has been outspoken about the need to ban composite sticks. In fact, he says that every coach in the National Hockey League would like to see them banned. Reflecting on his days as a player, he says that if a stick had broken and cost him a scoring chance—something that often happens with composite sticks—he would never again have used a stick of that type.*

* * *

As you probably know, I get a lot of bad write-ups in the papers.

I remember my very first bad write-up was after about a year on *Hockey Night in Canada*. You sort of get a honeymoon with the press.

But after about a year, a guy really gave it to me. I forget what it was. I think it was the usual thing—how I'm too right wing and all that stuff and how I wasn't good on television and my English.

Boy, I'll tell you. It was my very first one, and it really rocks you. It really did. You have to be pretty good to come back strong. It took me a couple of weeks to come back. I couldn't understand it.

But you get used to it after a while. I've had some tough ones.

I had one guy, when I was with the Mississauga Ice Dogs, attack my family, if you can believe it. I tell ya, that was a tough time when I was coaching Mississauga.

There's a reporter at the *Toronto Star*, he gives the good, the bad and the ugly every week. I think I made the good once, but I've made the bad and the ugly many, many times.

There was one female reporter in the *Toronto Sun*, she listed ten things and I can remember some of them.

One was that I was Neanderthal. I guess that's a bad guy, a prehistoric guy. I was a clown. A know-nothing. I was a pinhead. I know what that means. Barbarian. Blowhard. Troglodyte. I always remember troglodyte. I had to find out what that was. It's a cave dweller. And misogynist. I remember misogynist. I thought, "What the heck is that? Does she think I massage people?"

It was fear of women. There were some others, but I can't remember them. She called me a redneck. I was very happy with redneck because rednecks are the people who came over first to Canada and built Canada—the English, Irish and Scots. They were workin' on construction and in the fields, labouring ten hours a day, bent over so much that the back of their necks got red.

So to call me a redneck, I'm proud of it because that means a person who works ten hours a day in the sun. Works! You know what that is? Some people in Canada have forgotten what it means.

So I don't mind now when I get ripped in the paper—which I do quite a bit—because there's nothing more that can be said. There absolutely isn't. Everything that can be said has been said. Especially about my English, they love that.

But let me tell you, when you first get into this business, you have to be tough to survive.

* * *

Bobby Orr, to get ready for a game, would leave for the arena at two o'clock in the afternoon. The first time I saw it was on the Island.

I'm comin' in. I ate by myself in the afternoon. I'm comin' into the hotel and Bobby is standin' outside.

I said, "Hi Bobby, how are ya doin'?"

"Hi."

I'm telling ya, day of a game, he was like a lion.

I says, "Where are you goin'?"

"I'm goin' to the game."

Well, obviously, he didn't want to say anythin'. And I didn't want to say anythin'. I was just a rookie coach. It's two o'clock in the afternoon.

But he used to go down there to get ready. He used to get in the room and he had a stick with pucks taped to the blade on each side with a ton of tape on it. And he'd walk around with this all afternoon like he was a baseball player walkin' around with a lead bat, so that when he played, the stick would feel light.

The next time I saw this was in the 1976 Canada Cup. Guess who was down there that early gettin' ready for the game? Guy Lafleur and Bobby Clarke!

They were like lions. It's early afternoon and Guy's smokin' and gettin' ready for the game.

I see the guys now an hour before the game, they're out playin' soccer in the halls, out havin' a good time and laughin'. It's not quite the same as tigers like Orr, Lafleur and Clarke.

Maybe that's why they're in the Hall of Fame.

* * *

One of the best was when we were in Washington. We're on the bus goin' out to the rink in Landover, and Bobby Schmautz comes up and mentions a name. He said, "Go back and check on this guy."

So I go back and here's this guy reading *How to Be a Chartered Accountant.*

I says, "What are ya doin'?"

He says, "I'm just readin' a book, Grapes."

I says, "You're getting ready for the game, readin' *How to Be a Chartered Accountant?* The way you're playin' and the way you're goin', you'd better keep readin' that book, because that's what you're gonna end up as."

Imagine! A guy getting on the bus, gettin' ready for a game and he's readin' *How to Be a Chartered Accountant!*

You'll never be like Bobby Orr or Bobby Clarke or Guy Lafleur that way.

* * *

We'd won the Calder Cup in Rochester and we're having a party that night. Rose and I and Darryl Sly and his wife Sylvia are downstairs havin' fun and the whole deal and everything, and all of a sudden, the team doctor, Dr. Lorti, come down and says, "Come upstairs, quick! A player is after Joe because he didn't play him in the finals and he's grabbin' him and threatening him."

I say, "What do I care? Joe didn't play *me* much either. What do I care?"

He said, "You gotta come up."

So I gotta come up, and there's Red Armstrong. He's got a hold of Joe Crozier the coach, and so I gotta jump in.

I didn't want to be a hero, but what are you gonna do? So I jump in, and I always remember grabbing Red by his white shirt and all the buttons popped off. So I grab him and haul him back.

I says, "What are you doin'? Are you, nuts? You're gonna get suspended," and everything like that.

So I kinda threw him the other way, which kinda bugged me 'cause I liked Red. Now I'm back downstairs enjoyin' myself and Joe's leavin' to go home. Red says, "I'm comin' over to your house to get ya!"

So now Dr. Lorti comes down and says, "You have to go over and make sure nothing happens."

I says, "Are you crazy? I'm havin' a party with the guys. We just won."

He says, "Yeah, you have to go over there."

So Darryl Sly and I went over to sit in front of the house with a few pops and had to wait and see if Red was comin' over to kill Joe.

By that time I was wishin' he would. Just kiddin' Joe.

* * *

Joe was a pretty good guy. I was unemployed that summer, and I was still ticked at him because I didn't play in the finals, either.

He asked me, 'cause I was unemployed, if I'd paint his house. So he lowballed me on the job, but I needed the money and I painted his house. Somehow I made a mistake in the paint. I got a call from Joe saying, "This paint is all peeling."

Gosh I wonder how that happened?

* * *

After we won the Calder Cup in Rochester, Joe Crozier went out to Vancouver and ran the Canucks. Rochester was owned by Joe, and Vancouver was owned by Joe and Punch Imlach. One was in the American league and the other was in the Western league.

The Canucks were struggling, so he took half our Calder Cup champions out to Vancouver and left the rest of us to slug it out in Rochester. But he wasn't doin' very good out there, so Darryl Sly kept sayin' to him, "Bring out Cherry. Bring out Cherry. If you want us to go anywhere, bring out Cherry to play with me."

So finally, with two months to go in the season, Joe says, "You have to come out here."

. I says, "I don't want to go out there and leave my family." We had a lousy club in Rochester, but I didn't want to leave Rose and the kids.

He says, "It'll only be for a while." Well, you know this little thing, "for a while." You know how that goes.

So I go out there and I get in the Admiral Hotel and I'm roomin' with another defenceman by the name of Marc Reaume. Jim McKenny was livin' in the Admiral Hotel, too.

The great old Admiral Hotel! We used to go downstairs at night and watch the fights. It was the biggest tavern you ever saw in your life. There'd be fights and bartenders throwin' guys out every night.

So I'm out there in Vancouver, and I knew we weren't goin' to finish any higher than second spot, so we didn't have to worry too much.

We had Andy Bathgate. And Joe loved Andy Bathgate. He loved anybody that had played in the National Hockey League. Anybody that had played in the National Hockey League was a god to him because, let's face it, we were minor-leaguers.

Andy Bathgate had a habit. When he was skatin' around and we were warmin' up, he'd come around behind you and bang you on the behind with his stick and say, "Come on. Come on. Let's get goin'."

Well, I don't like anybody touchin' me with a stick. So the first practice, he did that to me. He come up and banged me from behind and said, "Come on, let's get goin'." I guess him being an NHL guy, he was goin' to show us minor-leaguers.

So I let him skate past me and get ahead, and I took my stick like an axe and I hit him about three times. Being in the National Hockey League didn't mean anything to me.

I said, "If you ever touch me again with that stick, you're gettin' it over the head next time."

He didn't.

* * *

Andy had this thing goin' where they were buying mining stocks. One of them was called Silver Arrow and everybody was into it.

Before practices, they were phonin' up. "How's Silver Arrow Mining doin'?"

Before the games, they were all worried about Silver Arrow. They were more worried about Silver Arrow than the game!

So I got up in the dressing room and I says, the next time I hear "Silver Arrow," somebody's gonna get it.

It never got mentioned again. Not while I was around, anyway.

Maybe I was jealous. I couldn't afford any stocks.

* * *

So we go into the playoffs, and that's when I turned it around. You can check on it. I think I was one of the leading scorers on the team. We went through the whole division.

I really didn't care at the time. We were playing Seattle and they had a great big defenceman, Don Ward, I think it was.

We had a real star, but he was terrified of this Don Ward. We were doin' nothin', so finally I turned to Joe on the bench and I said, "Get that so-and-so off the ice."

He says, "What did you say?"

I says, "You heard what I said. Get him off the ice. He doesn't want to play. He's terrified."

I didn't care because I was there for two months. We were in the playoffs and I wanted to win and get home.

So we kept goin' and we went through and we never lost a game all through the playoffs. We go up 3–0 in the final series and we're playin' the Portland Buckaroos.

As we're goin' off the ice, Joe comes to me and he says, "You've got to get to these guys. They think they've won it already."

I says, "Joe, I really don't care. I just want to win these games and get home."

He says, "You gotta straighten them out."

I says, "Why do I have to be the one to straighten 'em out? I don't give a damn what they do."

So I had to go in and act like a big hero. I threw down a bottle. I remember it was a bottle of 7-Up. I said, "We gotta win another game. We haven't won anything yet," and all that BS.

For some reason, even though we never lost a game in the playoffs and it was always a packed house in the Coliseum, they never liked us. We were winnin' and they were still booin' us for some reason. I guess it was because we were all from the east.

They were booin' us one night and I stood up on the bench and turned to them and I said, "Listen, we got one thing over you guys. We're gettin' out of this town once the season's over."

So anyhow, we did win the championship and never lost a game.

Two years later, the Canucks went into the National Hockey League and that team wasn't as good as the one we won with in the Western Hockey League.

* * *

One bad thing I remember after we won the championship.

After the game, the trainer said, "Okay, everybody take your skates off for the celebration."

Marc Reaume, he had scored the winning goal and he had been outside doin' an interview and he came inside with his skates on and stepped on a player's foot for fifty-two stitches.

The blood was all over the place. That sort of put a damper on the celebration.

But not for long.

* * *

After we'd won it all in Vancouver, I'm sittin' there and I said to Darryl, "You know, Darryl, once you win the championship and you take your equipment off, it's all over."

He said, "You know, what we should do is just sit here in our equipment."

So everybody else got dressed and showered and went to the party, and we sat in our equipment and never took it off for about three hours. The trainer come over and he said, "I'm leaving. Here. Here's two bottles of champagne." So we sat there and drank the two bottles of champagne.

Little did I know at the time, that was the last time I really played.

I'd won two championships in a row, and four in five years, but somehow, I had a feeling, and that's why I sat there with Darryl.

It was kinda sad. I wasn't hurt. I could still have played. I was in good shape. I'd worked on construction.

But Joe wouldn't take my calls, and it was my pride again. It had me retire, when I really should have played another two or three years.

* * *

What happened was, the year before, I was playing for Joe Crozier. As you know, he was the general manager and coach of the Rochester Americans. I was in his office one day, and I remember a player kept phonin' and he kept saying, "Aw, tell him I'll phone him later," and he kinda laughed at the guy, and I said to myself, "If he ever does that to me, I'm gonna retire."

Well, sure enough, after we won the championships and everythin', I kept phonin' Crozier. And I'm thinkin', "He's doin' to me what he did to the other guy."

All I wanted to know was what camp I was going to. I wanted to stay in Rochester, naturally. We had Tim and Cindy and we had to get them started at school.

I'd won four championships in five years and I can't get a call. So I quit.

I could easily have played two or three more years. I had no injuries and I was always in good shape from workin' on construction.

Joe phoned me a couple of weeks later like nothin' had happened and said, "Where would you like to play, Donnie?"

But my pride kept me retired. Pride goes before the fall, as they say—as I was to find out.

* * *

I went back to Rochester and kept working in Rochester on construction, doing the jackhammer and all that, and I was as happy as a pig in mud. You know how it goes—work all week, and on Friday night have a few pops with my good friend Whitey Smith.

But unfortunately, I got laid off, and when I got laid off, it was tough, tough sleddin'. This is in the seventies. I started a job where I worked eight hours a day and got $16. Two dollars an hour, I was makin'. People on welfare were makin' more money.

* * *

I went to the unemployment office—and the lady was nice; I'm not knockin' her—with the rest of the guys that got laid off from construction. She was nice, but she was askin' personal questions— How much money you got? The whole deal.

I said, "Thank you very much, ma'am."

She said, "Well, don't take offence." She was a nice lady and I think she felt sorry for me.

I said, "No, I'm not takin' offence. I'll try it some other way." So, like I say, I painted for two dollars an hour. They knew you had to take the job. It was pretty tough.

So Valley Cadillac in Rochester saw a little value in me. I had been captain of the Rochester Americans a couple of years ago, so they thought they could make a Cadillac salesman out of me.

I proceeded to be the worst Cadillac salesman ever in the world. There's no doubt about it.

When one guy said to me, "All you Cadillac salesmen are alike," I nailed him against the wall, so I know I was not one of the happiest.

I was very, very unhappy. I made some good money and drove a Cadillac, but I was very unhappy because I knew I wasn't doing the job and I was stealin' my salary.

I was laying in bed one day having a nap, and I said to myself, "You know, you don't even deserve a nap."

I'm hurryin' this through, but this actually happened. I got on my knees beside the bed and I said, "Is this it, Lord? I've worked hard all my life, did the best I could, always was honest. Is this the end of the line for me at thirty-six?"

And I know some people won't believe this, but a voice or some-thin' came to me. The room seemed to get brighter—and I'm not an evangelist or anything like that—but a voice told me, "You quit the Cadillac and you make a comeback in hockey."

I drove down and turned in my Cadillac and the general man-ager said, "Don, I was going to phone you this week and tell you you're not cut out to be a Cadillac salesman—or any car salesman. You just don't have it."

I phoned the Rochester Americans. It was the middle of the sum-mer and Doug Adams—he was the coach and GM at the time and he lived in North Carolina—just happened to be in for a day. I said, "Can I come down and see you for ten minutes?"

He says, "I guess so." That's all he said was, "I guess so." He didn't seem too happy.

So I asked him if I could make a comeback. He thought, "Well, here's this fat guy sittin' there, an old guy. It'd be good PR givin' an old guy a chance."

So he said, "Okay, I'll give you a chance. You can come to the training camp."

I'm twenty pounds overweight. So I stopped drinkin' beer. I got a rubber suit. In the middle of summer, I ran in a rubber suit.

I got on my stationary bicycle and turned the tension down as hard as you could. It was burnt rubber. You could smell it all over.

When it wasn't hot outside, I went up in the attic with the bike. It was hotter in the attic and I wanted to make sure I'd lose some weight. Rose came to me one day and said, "You're going to die of a heart attack."

I said, "That's right, Rose. I'm either gonna die or I'm gonna make this club."

* * *

So I cut down on the weight and I'm in pretty good shape and I come to the rink and here I am, the captain of the Calder Cup winners and all that, and the trainer put me in with the rookies.

I remember he gave me gloves that were all full of holes. I looked at him and he just shrugged.

He paid for it, but that's another story. So I tried out and I was not doin' bad. I was holdin' my own and doin' pretty good and everythin', but it just wasn't there.

I'm getting better and better, but in hockey, there's a certain flow, or a certain feel—something that you know. But I hadn't nailed it down. It just wasn't there.

So I'm playing exhibition games and I can hold my own because of my experience and everythin', but it just wasn't there.

I remember we had an exhibition game—the Rochester Americans against the Springfield Indians in Stratford, Ontario.

I phoned Rose from the hallway before the game and I said, "You know, Rose, I'm doin' all right, but I just can't seem to nail it down. It's just not comin'."

She said, "Well, you can't quit now. You gotta give it another game anyhow."

And during that exhibition game in Stratford—I remember it was an old rink—and during that game, it came to me.

It was beautiful! What a feeling it was to have that feeling back again! So I'm all set to go. I'm so excited to start the season. The Rochester Americans were gonna start the season in Cincinnati, Ohio, playing the Swords. They were called that because they were the farm team of the Buffalo Sabres. Get it?

So anyhow, I'm all set. Adams calls me over. It was just before the game, in the lobby of the hotel. They had a rule in the American Hockey League, you could only dress six guys over the age of twenty-six. Well, I was the seventh guy. I never was so disappointed in my life.

I was so pumped, you couldn't believe. Then he told me that.

I was kinda choked up. I had to go over and look in the window where they had those little Hummel figures. I let on I was looking at them so no one would see me all choked up.

We go to the game. They get hammered 8–1. Let me tell you somethin': when you're sitting out, don't ever let anyone give you the idea that they're happy when the team wins. When they get hammered 8–1 and you're not playin', you're happy. That's the truth.

* * *

So I played the next game. It's in Cleveland. We lose, but I get two points and I'm picked as one of the stars. We play the next game. I forget where it was, but I get a goal. That's three points now in two games, and I'm the highest plus on the team.

We come home; then in the next game, we tie 3–3. I remember blastin' a shot from the point and a player called Jimmy Wiste tippin' it and it goes in the top corner and we tied it 3–3.

I got two points in that game. Now I had five points in three games. I led the team in hits. I led the team in scoring—and I was a defenceman. And I was the highest plus. That was Sunday night.

I was absolutely in heaven. I lead the team in all those departments and everything. Then I get a call late that night that I was not making the trip south, not even going on the bus, because I was over twenty-six.

He was doin' it again! You'll never, ever believe how bad I felt. A lot of people ask, "Why were you so upset when that Kris Newbury kid got sent down?" I did a big thing on him with the Leafs on "Coach's Corner."

If you remember, what happened was, he came up from the Marlies, had a terrific fight, got a goal, they beat the Canadiens right in Montreal, and he was picked one of the three stars. He got a goal and he was told the next morning he was going back to the minors.

It's so unfortunate that you would treat a human being like that. But nobody but Kris and me were upset. I knew how he felt because I'd had that hurt.

I'd never forgotten what happened to me in Rochester. That was one of the great disappointments in my life. After that, I kept playin' and got in the lineup once in a while, but when you're old like that and you don't play regular, you don't take a regular shift, you get out of shape awful fast and you lose it. So it was tough.

I rode out the rest of the year and I got made coach. But that's another story.

* * *

In hockey, you have a code. First of all, never hit a guy when he's down.

And second of all, when you see a kid can't fight, you stop.

The only time I ever went against that policy, it was Mike McMahon and my conscience bothered me afterwards. He was just a kid, playin' for Baltimore, I think.

I didn't know who he was and it was right in front of their bench. He cross-checked me headfirst into the boards.

Well, I come up underneath and around. Now I'm on top of him and I'm not at all thrilled about being piled headfirst into the boards, so it was just automatic. I drilled him and I knocked all his front teeth out.

I didn't know I'd done it at the time, but the team doctor, Dr. Lorti, told me the next day that he had to go and get oral surgery. I found out that his dad was there at the game. His dad, Mike Sr., played for Montreal during the war. The Quebec Aces, too. What a bummer.

That's when I started to get a conscience: after I saw this kid there with all his teeth knocked out. And once you start to get a conscience as a fighter, you're not gonna fight as good because you're gonna hesitate.

As soon as you hesitate, you lose that jump and you're done.

I was about thirty-four at the time, and once you get about thirty-four, you don't quite seem to have that spark to fight. I didn't have it anymore, sad.

* * *

I'm gonna jump ahead. Now I'm coachin' for Rochester and I end up with Mike McMahon on my team.

We've never mentioned that incident, but I always had parties and Rose always put parties on for the players and the wives. We were the party place, even though I was the coach.

I'm talkin' to the guys in the kitchen and I'm sayin', "Listen, you guys, if you're gonna fight, get the first one in and make it a good one."

And Mike is sittin' at our kitchen table and he laughs and says, "Yeah Grapes, I know all about that," and he clicked his dentures.

* * *

There was a time, maybe about five or six years ago, when it started to get on my nerves that any place I went, there was always a crowd and I had to sign autographs.

Then I started thinking, "You should feel honoured that people want to ask you for an autograph, big-timer, jerk."

What happened was I saw one of the guys signing autographs and he wasn't lookin' at the guy. Hockey players are usually very good, but this guy was signin' an autograph and he was talkin' to someone else. He didn't even look at the kid who asked for the autograph.

I thought, "Wait a minute! Something is wrong here."

I said to myself, "You've got to smarten up. All those years that you were in those minor leagues, and now you're starting to think you don't have to do it. That could be Timothy or Cindy asking for that autograph."

So I try to treat every person as if it was Cindy or Tim asking for an autograph.

It doesn't bother me at all. I came around. I was startin' to fall into that rut of just scribbling somethin'. Now, usually I ask who they'd like it to and all that.

I was walking through the airport with a guy from Cold-FX and people are saying, "Hey Grapes, how's it goin'?"

And the guy with me says, "You know, it's the strangest thing. I've been with you for two days now. It seems all these guys that holler, it seems like they're your buddies, all these baggage guys and everybody."

He said, "It's like they all know you." That made me feel good.

Here's another thing. Sixty percent of the people who come up and ask for autographs are women. Every girl loves a sharp-dressed man.

(Actually, they're usually asking for an autograph for their husband or boyfriend.)

* * *

At one time, a long time ago, they tried to move "Coach's Corner" to the second intermission, but they got a lot of complaints from parents who said they let their kids stay up to watch "Coach's Corner" and then they have to go to bed. If it was the second intermission, it was too late.

I know when I go to the arenas for the minor-midget games—which I do a lot and which I love going to, by the way—I'll see a parent holdin' a kid who is so small he can hardly walk.

So this is not a setup. And as I come by, they'll say to the little baby, "Who's that?"

And the kid will put up his thumb.

* * *

Another time, we're on a plane and we're sittin' together and this couple gets on—a guy with a good-looking girl.

I had an idea that she didn't know who we were, but the guy must have sent her up to get our autographs. It was a small business-class section, and Ron had the window seat to my right and I was sittin' on the aisle.

She says, "Well, Don, could you give me your autograph and make it 'To Tony'?"

I said, "Oh yeah," and I had an idea she didn't know who Ron was. I hesitated. Usually, I just put the card over to him to sign, but this time I hesitated and said, "Do you want him to sign it?"

She said, "Oh. Are you somebody?" The whole business class laughed.

Ron laughed. He thinks it's funny. He didn't at one time, but now he thinks it's funny.

* * *

Ron never forgave me for what I did the night the picture of him wearing a top hat was taken. The picture is in the book.

It was the last game in Maple Leaf Gardens and Ron had to introduce all the former Toronto players who were there. It was a tough job because he had to introduce over a hundred guys and he was getting weak by the end. The only guy in worse shape was the bagpiper who played for every guy who came out. Ron said his face was turning purple.

But what ticked Ron off was that before he went out, he asked me how he looked in the top hat and I said, "Good."

He gets kidded about it even to this day.

It started right away. The cartoon in *The Globe and Mail* the next day showed Ron from behind wearing his top hat and a sign that said, "Kick me."

A funny thing happened a few years later. We were with NHL commissioner Gary Bettman and Ron was giving him a hard time as usual.

Out of a clear blue sky, Gary said, "Oh well, some guys can't wear a hat."

* * *

When I was a little boy, my mom would buy Quaker Oats, and back in those days, they'd give you eight-by-ten glossies of the NHL players.

Later on, Bee Hive Corn Syrup gave you those little cardboard ones, but the eight-by-ten glossies were absolutely gorgeous.

Maurice Richard, "The Rocket," had the best picture of all. I've never seen it since. The photographer stood up on the bench and took it lookin' down. And the Rocket is lookin' up at him with those eyes. It's like they have fire in them.

I remember Babe Pratt, there was a picture of him, too. Babe was a friend of mine, and I hope he doesn't mind me tellin' this story if he's lookin' down.

The Leafs were playin' the championship game and Babe went to block a shot. The puck went between his legs and went in for the winning goal. So they're all in the dressing room with their heads down and Major Conn Smythe, the owner of the Maple Leafs, is walking around.

It's silent and they're all afraid to say somethin' because Conn is in one of his moods.

Like I said, Babe had gone to block the shot, but the puck had gone between his legs and went in. He says, "Conn, I guess I shoulda closed my legs."

And Conn says, "No, *you* shouldn't have closed your legs. Your mother should have closed *her* legs."

AL'S NOTE: *Babe Pratt was one of hockey's legendary characters. He played twelve years in the NHL for New York Rangers, Toronto and Boston. His son Tracy played for ten years with six teams.*

Babe was a gregarious guy and a tremendous after-dinner speaker. After his playing career ended, he spent a lot of time in various capacities, mostly unofficial, for the Vancouver Canucks.

The last time I saw him, he was at a Canucks training camp in 1988, and he didn't look particularly healthy.

I asked him how he was doing and his answer was typical. "Well, let's put it this way," he said. "I told my wife not to buy me any green bananas."

He died three months later.

* * *

Babe posed great in the Quaker pictures, but the one picture I always had beside me and looked at every night when I went to bed was Kenny Reardon. It was a colour picture in *Sport* magazine. Remember *Sport* magazine?

I cut that picture out and put it on the wall and every night, I'd go to bed, sleepin' in my bunk bed with my brother above, looking at the picture of Kenny Reardon.

I'll tell you how much I loved Kenny Reardon. In the newsreels back in those days, you'd get about three minutes of hockey. So we'd go to the movies and sit through the shows just to see the three minutes of hockey.

So there was about three seconds of Kenny Reardon, and I sat there through three shows just to see Kenny Reardon skatin' up the ice.

He was my hero of heroes. He was playin' in Montreal and was he tough!

Him and Cal Gardner, who I played with later, had a thing goin' throughout their careers. One time, Gardner cross-checked Reardon in the mouth and Reardon swore that he would get even. In those days, players never forgot grudges.

Every time they played against each other, they battled until finally, Kenny Reardon broke Gardner's jaw.

After that, Mr. Campbell made Kenny Reardon put up a $1000 peace bond to make sure he wouldn't hurt him. That was the only way he could keep Gardner safe. Although Cal didn't need any protection. Him and a defenceman called Pete Goegan had one of the best fights I ever saw. Cal could give it out. Cal could take it.

The funny thing is that when Cal went to the hospital to get his face worked on, that was where he met the woman he later married. Cal told me it was worth the broken jaw to meet his wife.

AL'S NOTE: *Clarence Campbell was the president of the NHL from 1946 to 1978 and a highly respected man throughout the league. He had been a lawyer representing the Canadian Army at the Nuremberg war crime trials following the Second World War.*

* * *

Kenny Reardon was my hero of heroes and I had played against his brother Terry. Terry had played in Providence and coached in

Baltimore. So the only Reardon I really knew was Terry.

When I was in the Canadiens camp, I was on the bench in practice, and we were havin' a scrimmage and Gary Bergman was sittin'
beside me and Kenny Reardon come up behind the bench and said,
"Don, welcome to the camp. Thank you very much for comin'."

And I turned around fast and he looked just like his brother and
I said, "Thanks very much, Terry."

All my life, I wanted to meet Kenny Reardon. He has been my
hero for twenty years and the first time I meet him, I call him Terry!

I didn't know I'd called him Terry, and Gary Bergman says, "I
wouldn't do that again, Don, if I were you."

And I says, "Why?"

He says, "Because that was Kenny and you just called him Terry."

I felt bad.

* * *

But I'll tell you what kind of guy Kenny Reardon was. We were way
up north doin' an exhibition game, and was it cold!

There were two kids who were tryin' out for the team and they
didn't have coats.

We were in a department store and Kenny Reardon came in and
saw these two kids and saw they had no coats and said, "Give these
two kids coats and give me the bill."

He was in the Second World War and he got a letter of com-
mendation. He was a motorcycle dispatch rider, one of the most
dangerous jobs of all because the Germans knew they'd be carryin'
important information, so they'd try to pick them off.

He was my hero and he's still my hero.

AL'S NOTE: *Kenny Reardon joined the Canadian Army in 1942 and went
overseas in 1943. In Canada at that time, no one was posted overseas without having volunteered to do so. Reardon won the Field Marshall
Montgomery Award of Merit for several acts of bravery in battle. He returned*

to the Canadiens in 1946, but retired in 1950 at the age of twenty-nine. He died March 15, 2008.

* * *

When we had training camp, all the rookies come in. They all thought they were somethin', but I'd call 'em in and say, "Look, you do what you want with Cashman. You want to take O'Reilly on, or John Wensink or Stan Jonathan, or Al Secord, or anybody else you want to take on, you can take them on.

"But the one guy you don't even look at sideways is Bobby Schmautz, the little guy over there with the big nose. Don't even look at him, because he'll cut you if you give him a hard time."

I saw him one time in Detroit, when a guy give him a hard time — a young defenceman called Jean Hamel, and he was just a kid. He knocked Schmautzie down and I knew what was comin'.

I said, "Schmautzie, give the kid a break."

Not a chance. Schmautzie's eyes were twirling and I watched him and I didn't even see him cut the kid. But he did it. That's how good he was with the stick. He was terrifying.

* * *

I was giving a morning speech about something to the team one time and Schmautzie interrupted me and said that I was overweight.

I can't remember the circumstances, but I said, "True, Schmautzie. I'm overweight. But I can lose twenty pounds whereas you can't grow a foot."

* * *

Schmautzie was always talking about the Germans, and one day, he come out to practice and he had drawn a big Iron Cross on the back of his practice sweater.

The Bruins' owner, Jeremy Jacobs, was Jewish. Figure it out. Harry Sinden went nuts.

So I call Schmautzie over and tell him that he's got to get rid of the sweater. But being Schmautzie, he has to argue and start telling me how great the Germans are.

While he's doing this, Cashman skates over and says, "Germans are great, only they can't finish what they start."

Schmautzie looks at me and says, "Can't argue about that."

And that was the end of it.

* * *

One time in Vancouver, when they used to have the low glass, we're in a game and Schmautzie came over and asked what I wanted him to do.

His eyes were twirlin', and I remember there was a father and son sittin' right behind us, and I could hear them.

The boy says, "Dad, look at that man's eyes. Look at that man's eyes!"

And the father says, "Oh, that's just Bobby Schmautz."

I never understood this. In his last year he had 27 goals. He had 61 points. Twenty-seven goals and he couldn't get a job the next year!

Harry Neale—he was the general manager and coach of the Vancouver Canucks, which was the last team Schmautzie played for—wouldn't invite him back because he was hard to handle.

He was his own worst enemy. He was a guy who would take up the cause of anyone who was in trouble. *He* was trouble, and I loved him. I wish I could have a team of 20 Schmautzies, I'd never lose.

* * *

You must realize that back in the fifties—the early fifties—the Barrie Flyers were a dynasty, and everybody wanted to play for Hap

Emms because Hap Emms was the best coach in junior hockey.

He was also one of the meanest men I've ever met in my life—meaner than Shore, which is hard to believe.

We had such a good team when I played for them in the 1952–53 season that they called us the best team money could buy, 'cause he went out and bought the best players off other teams. He went down and got them and promised people things. We went out and got the best goalie and the best everything.

We played in front of 16,000 people in Maple Leaf Gardens and they played that tune, the *Dragnet* theme, that dum-da-dum-dum. It was a theme song for a TV series about crime and people felt we stole the players.

We went through and won the championship the way it should be. First of all, we beat St. Mike's. Then we beat the Toronto Marlboros.

But let's talk about the St. Mike's one first. We were smokin' 'em. Billy Dineen, one of the nicest guys you'll ever meet in your life, was the captain. He is the salt of the earth.

Near the end of the game, we were smokin' 'em and Charlie Cerre was the coach of the other team. Hap got somethin' all wrapped up as a present and he calls over Billy Dineen during a stoppage.

He says, "Will you give this as a token of my esteem to Coach Cerre?"

We're thinkin', "Oh, he never did that before. That's nice."

So Billy takes it over and Charlie Cerre opened it up on the bench—and it was a book: *How to Coach Hockey*.

Billy Dineen went nuts. He come runnin' over and tried to get into our bench.

Hap Emms just laughed.

AL'S NOTE: *The* Dragnet *theme was heard everywhere in the 1950s. The original version, as recorded by Ray Anthony, reached No. 2 on the Billboard charts in 1952.*

* * *

In the next round, we're playing the Marlies. Everybody in Toronto hated the Marlies, 'cause they always got leather jackets, the best equipment, and the best sweaters. The Leafs treated them first class, and it's still a first class organization. Hap Emms was so cheap that all we had was second-hand equipment. We even had equipment that Eddie Shore wore. All our socks had holes in 'em. We didn't even get tape to hold them up. We had to use strips of rubber tubing that was cut from old discarded inner tubes.

So we hated the Marlies, but so did everybody else. They were so good, the organization, with their leather jackets and their practisin' in the Gardens, that everybody hated them.

We were beatin' 'em, and with five minutes to go, Hap Emms told us we could not go over the red line. We had to pass the puck around.

Naturally, they got mad and ran us, and they were down two men the whole time. We still couldn't go over the red line. We had to keep passin' the puck around. The crowd was laughin' at them. We couldn't fight back. We had to let them run at us and the crowd laughed at them—16,000 people laughin' at you in your home rink.

That's when they put the rule in that you had to advance the puck. That's how mean Hap Emms was.

* * *

Then we went and played the Quebec Citadelles in Quebec.

In Quebec, in the eastern Canadian finals, we lost the first game, and the headline was that the reason we lost was that our heads were so big we couldn't get inside the rink.

We did not like Hap, but he was so good. We won the series and then we went out west and played the St. Boniface Canadiens. We were playin' longer than the Stanley Cup playoffs.

We were up 3–0 in the series and he asked us to do one thing. "Three years ago we won it four straight, if we win tonight that means I've won the Memorial Cup in four straight games without a loss twice, it has never been done before."

We lost.

We won the next game easily, and we won the Cup. I often wonder if we did that to spite Hap.

* * *

Hap Emms went on from Barrie to Niagara Falls. Then in 1965 he went on to the National Hockey League.

He was the first guy to sign Bobby Orr to an NHL contract. He was the GM of the Bruins at the time.

He signed Bobby Orr on his yacht for $100,000. They almost lost Bobby because of Hap. He was always cheap and he didn't want to give him that much money.

The Bruins' owner said, "You'd *better* sign him."

So he did. But if it had been up to Hap, they would have lost him.

Hap was mean and cheap, but he was the smartest coach I ever played for, and you feared him, and I'll admit I respected him, he was a hockey guy through and through.

* * *

When I was a player, in the morning, I used to have my tea and honey. I used to go for a morning skate. I'd have my steak. I'd have my nap and I'd go to the game dopey.

You see the players walkin' into the rink and they always look dopey, like they've just woke up. The reason is they've just woke up.

They have to have their nap and they have to have their vanilla ice cream with chocolate sauce. You see them goin' to their rooms in the hotels, they'll take their ice cream and eat it in their room before their nap.

They'll watch a little television—the soap operas. That's how Gretzky got to be on *The Young and the Restless*, because he watched it before he had a nap. They have to have their nap.

I did the same as a player. I'd have my nap and go to the game dopey. Then when I coached, I did the exact same thing. Don't bother me the afternoon of a game. I see guys now out there runnin' and stuff like that, but don't bother me the afternoon of the game.

"Coach's Corner" is the very same way. I have my steak. I have my nap. Don't bother me. I go in there and I'm a little dopey.

When I come in, I'm half-asleep and I have three cups of coffee on an empty stomach, 'cause I ate at 12:30, and when it's time to do "Coach's Corner," I'm ready to go. I'm just like the players and think like the players.

* * *

I used to drive to the home games, but I have to have somebody drive me in now.

When the Leafs played at Maple Leaf Gardens, people started to follow me, and I'd park my truck and they'd be waitin' around my truck or my '83 Lincoln after the game.

It got to the point that I couldn't get in my car.

Finally, a policeman came by and he said, "Look, Don, this is ridiculous. We know people like you a lot, but all there has to be is one kook out there waitin' for you because everybody knows your truck now. And everybody knows where you park."

So I feel kind of guilty now takin' a limo in, but I have to. It's not that I want to. I like drivin' my Lincoln, but I have to have a limo.

So we drive in and I get out and I'm like a hockey player before the game. Don't fool with me before "Coach's Corner."

AL'S NOTE: *It is made very clear to everyone working on the show, even those of us who do the "Hot Stove" segment during the second intermission, that Don is to be left alone until "Coach's Corner" has finished.*

Studio 42, where both shows are done, is on the tenth floor of the CBC building in downtown Toronto. Prior to their show, the second-intermission people sit in the fifth-floor office of Sherali Najak, the executive producer of Hockey Night in Canada.

There are three TVs in there, and we watch the first periods of three games, then "Coach's Corner."

After that, we head upstairs for makeup, then go into the Lotus Room, the small room just off Studio 42, that Don and Ron use prior to their show. We tell Ron the general topics that will be up for discussion on the "Hot Stove." At that point, we chat with Don. But no sooner.

The Lotus Room, by the way, is just a little change room with a couple of amenities, but some years ago, Kelly Hrudey named it the Lotus Room after a bar he used to frequent. The name stuck.

* * *

After "Coach's Corner," I'm all right. It's just like a game—just like I'm coaching.

I build up for that "Coach's Corner." It's not like, "Oh well, here's 'Coach's Corner.'"

I build up to it.

Here's the strange thing. Ron MacLean lives fifteen minutes from my house. I'm in Mississauga and he is in Oakville, south of the Queen Elizabeth Way with all the rich people.

We travel in different circles. I never see him except Saturdays. Never.

I think we've found that it's better to be that way, because we've found that when we do get together on Saturday, we're ready to go. Whereas, if we were talkin' all the time, we could get worn down. And that's the way we like it.

When people ask, "How come you guys have lasted so long?" I say, "I have no idea."

If I knew what I was doing, I'd probably screw it up.

* * *

He phones me on Saturday morning at 9:30 and says, "What have you got for me? What are we gonna talk about?"

I might say, "I've got Savard. I've got Iginla." Boom. Boom. That's it. We never beat it to death.

I feel sorry for him. He goes in there at eleven and he's still goin' at ten after one in the morning.

That *Hockey Day in Canada*, when we're on location some- where in the country, he's on all day, startin' two hours before the first game, then doin' three games. I said, "You know, guys can do that just as smooth as you, but they could never do it with the joy that you do it with."

It was the one and only compliment I ever gave him. I must have been drinkin'.

I've been in the game a long time, and I can see that he really means what he says on *Hockey Day.* He does it and it's not a job to him.

I look at him and he's getting pushed and shoved around. We did that one show way up north, and it was seventy-one below and it froze the camera and he still loved it. He did it with joy. I don't understand it.

When he reads this, he won't believe it's me talkin', 'cause I never say anything like this to him. When we're on the road together, it's constant pecking at one another, trying to hurt one another.

Our thing is we try to make each other look bad. When we're on TV, he tries to make me look bad and I try to make him look bad.

Like if I show a sign of weakness with a cold, he says, "Have you got a cold? Have you got a cold?"

"No, I haven't got a cold."

I won't give him the satisfaction.

* * *

I must admit that when we're on the road in the playoffs during those two last months, we do drink a lot.

It's our thing to do, and how we ever keep goin', I don't know. We go from April 8 to June 9 every other night, and the last two series, when we're on the road, we do drink every other night.

I don't know whether it's a form of relaxation or what. We drink together, but except for each other's company, we drink alone.

* * *

Before we go to the game, we'd put twelve beers in a sink, or in a garbage pail, packed with ice, and leave them in the hotel room.

In the playoffs, we have hectic schedules and you get tired. Sometimes, I get really ticked off and I want to kill somebody. Believe me, in the playoffs, when you get tired, it's tough, and I really have said I'm gonna kill somebody if I can get a hold of him.

MacLean would see somethin' goin' on and he'd look at me and hold up six fingers. Then he'd say slowly, so I could read his lips, "Six. Cold. Waiting."

And I'd say, "Yeah, yeah, all right."

That was our thing. No matter how upset we'd get, we'd know there are those twelve cold beers waiting. With peanuts and cheese.

It's a way of life for us.

* * *

When we're on the road, he goes to the rink about two in the afternoon for a seven o'clock start. I would get there about 5:30, but we had to stop that because last year when I was in the play-offs in Vancouver, I got into a cab and the guy couldn't speak English.

He didn't even know where GM Place was, and he ended up parking me somewhere in Chinatown and I'm runnin' across highways and I got in just before "Coach's Corner."

But I don't get a limo on the road. I still take a cab, so someday, if I miss "Coach's Corner," you know I'm running around in a cab somewhere.

I'm going to have to talk to the bosses at *Hockey Night* and say I have to have a limo, because sometimes, the taxi drivers don't even know what I'm talkin' about when I tell them where I want to go.

* * *

I know that when he was in Los Angeles, Wayne Gretzky had to get a limo to take him to the games.

When I used to do banquets—I don't do them anymore—they used to want to send a limo for me. They'd drive me anywhere I wanted and I'd say "No," even if I had to go out of town. I'd always want to drive my car. But I had to stop.

And I understand Gretzky was the same way. When he'd go to a banquet or somethin', he'd want to be by himself, drivin'. And that's what I used to like about drivin', because you can think about what you're going to say and you're alone.

But sometimes, and I understand Gretzky did the same thing, you'd drive right by an exit.

So now we take limos.

* * *

Nancy Lee just didn't understand me.

She had lunch with me just before the 2004 World Cup of Hockey. I think she was trying to antagonize me to get me to quit.

So what happened was, we're havin' lunch and she says, "You're not doin' the World Cup. We're getting Brian Burke and Kelly Hrudey."

She's tryin' to get me to bite because I've always done those tournaments.

I said, "Okay, good."

So she didn't know how to react to that one. She thought I'd get mad and say, "Yeah, well, I'm quittin' if you don't."

But I didn't. I just said, "Yeah, okay."

So then she says to me, "This is your last year," and she looked at me for my reaction.

I says, "Yeah, okay. If that's the way you want it."

She just couldn't figure it out. She thought for sure, I'd say, "Shove it," but I just said, "Yeah, okay."

I just went along with it. I wasn't going to fight her on her terms. I was going to sit and think.

I had a meeting with one of the top suits at the CBC. I think this guy wanted it to be his legacy that he got rid of me. I think he and Nancy figured they had me gone.

I remember him saying that he'd get rid of me. And he said, "When the stuff hits the fan, I'll be retired on my island."

I said "Okay" and I just kept goin' along with it. I had a plan, don't worry. But I just kept goin' along with them.

Fortunately for me, Richard Stursberg came in. He's a bottom-line guy, evidently, and he cancelled their plans.

AL'S NOTE: *In 2000, Nancy Lee was named executive director of CBC Sports. She resigned from the position in 2006. Richard Stursberg's official title is executive vice-president of English services and head of CBC-TV English.*

* * *

I'm often asked, "Are you and Ron friends?"

We are, but we've had some awful arguments.

The one thing that I regret saying to him was when he was having a tough time with Colin Campbell.

What happens is you get so mentally tired in the playoffs and so caught up in it that you get punchy.

He'd said something to Colin he felt bad about, and then when I come on, he was tryin' to explain why he'd said what he did.

I said, "Aw, quit whinin'! Stand up and be a man. You said it. Stand by it." I got carried away. It really hurt him.

He was really mad at that one.

That's too bad. He makes me mad sometimes.

But that's the one thing I regret.

* * *

I've been in trouble a lot.

There was the one about the French and the visors. There was the one in the Olympics when Suzanne Tremblay said that the French-Canadians didn't like the Canadian flags all over the place and I said, "Well, we're payin' for it; if you don't like it, don't go," or somethin'.

Then there was the Iraq War, when Canada didn't back the United States.

Ron MacLean and I got goin' on that, and he wouldn't stop. The reason he wouldn't stop was that they were tellin' him to stop. And when you tell him to stop, that's just like a red flag in front of a bull and he wouldn't stop.

I really didn't want to get that deep into it, because I knew we were gettin' into trouble. But he wanted to keep goin', so I says, "Oh, okay, if you want to keep goin', let's go, and we'll all go down in flames."

It was back and forth, back and forth. I said, "We should back the United States. They backed us in two world wars."

I said, "It's like bein' in a bar with a friend. Even though you know your friend is wrong, when he gets in a fight, what are you going to do? Walk out and leave him and say he's wrong?"

It went on and on like that.

When that episode was over, everybody had left the studio. We were alone. And nobody said anything for two minutes.

Finally I turned to him and I said, "Did you really mean that BS?"

He says, "Yeah." I just shook my head because I figured we were both done there. I mean, really, I thought we were done. So did he.

AL'S NOTE: *In January 2004, Don was talking about visors and said, "Most of the guys that wear them are Europeans and French guys." There were a number of protests and the matter was investigated by the federal government—the Official Languages Commissioner, to be precise—at the taxpayers' expense. All that was really required to settle the matter was someone who could count. The majority of visor wearers in the NHL are French-Canadian and European.*

* * *

But the most trouble I got into was when the Persian Gulf War was on, and we were in Chicago Stadium. They were singin' the anthem and they had the sparklers goin', and back in Canada, they were burnin' the American flag.

I had taken an eight-foot Canadian flag to Chicago and I had put it up in back of us while we were doin' "Coach's Corner." I covered up the *Hockey Night in Canada* logo while I was doin' "Coach's Corner."

And what I said that really upset them was, "How come these kooks that burn the American flag are out there doin' it in the afternoon? Don't those creeps ever work?"

They just went nuts over that one back at the CBC. I guess they liked creeps. They just went crazy.

Alan Clark was the head of CBC Sports at the time. He come out and he was really upset. He says, "Just tell me! Tell me it wasn't premeditated!"

I says, "Oh no, Alan. I always carry an eight-foot Canadian flag in my pocket."

* * *

Did you ever hear the story and Donald Brashear and me in Vancouver?

Donald Brashear and I never got along. I always thought that he only fought middleweights.

I never forgave him for what he did to Marty McSorley. Marty had a bad shoulder and Brashear knew he couldn't fight. So then he did a number on Marty and did a hand-wiping motion as if he won the fight.

That's when Marty knew he couldn't fight and hit him with the stick. I still say he meant to hit him on the shoulder.

That's neither here nor there, but I had given Brashear a hard time on that.

So I here I am in Vancouver, and I don't know who he was with, but it was dark in the studio and I look up and he's standing right in front of the desk. Donald Brashear!

So I just nodded to him and said, "Hello."

He says, "You say 'Hello' to me, you dummy?"

I says, "You're calling me a dummy?"

He says, "Yeah," and we're going back and forth calling each other a dummy.

So now I said, "I've had enough."

I take off my mike and I'm comin' around the desk. "Let's go!"

I remember he had a nice brown suit on. And all of a sudden, it must have hit him: "What am I doin'? Here I am in the studio of *Hockey Night in Canada* and I'm about to get in a fistfight with Don Cherry."

So he turned and left and started to walk down the hall, and I'm hollerin', "You coward! Just like you did with Marty!"

So he did a funny thing. He really did a funny thing. He turned into a doorway, and as he was goin' in the door, he turned to me and zipped his finger across his mouth. It was pretty good.

I come back in the studio and I'm fumin'. I'm walkin' up and down the studio and I'm just fumin'. And when somethin' like that happens, everybody lets on that they're lookin' into a bag or somethin'. They don't want to make eye contact.

So MacLean is looking in his bag and I'm fumin', sayin', "You heard him call me a dummy. You heard him call me a dummy."

So MacLean, who always comes up with somethin', looks up and says, "Well, I don't know. I heard him sayin somethin' about honky."

So we all started laughin', and he broke the ice as he usually does.

AL'S NOTE: *The official version is that Marty McSorley was suspended for twenty-three games for whacking Brashear in the head with his stick.*

In fact, he was effectively suspended for life. The initial suspension took McSorley out for the remainder of the 1999–2000 season—twenty-three games. But in fact, the suspension was open-ended. It would have included the playoffs should McSorley be on a playoff-bound team. Furthermore, he would be required to apply for permission to be reinstated.

* * *

Dave Hodge really didn't want to do "Coach's Corner."

Dave Hodge did not particularly like me, and you could see it.

When Ron MacLean took over as the host of "Coach's Corner," what Hodge told him was, "Don't let Cherry pick the topics."

I thought that was kind of unfair. It's my show. And I'm only on for seven minutes.

For some reason he didn't like me. That's all I'm going to say about that.

* * *

When I first started to do "Coach's Corner" at Maple Leaf Gardens, I'd be tryin' to do somethin' serious and there'd be a guy pouring coffee for the makeup lady. I remember the one guy, he was a lighting guy or somethin', and he was tryin' to put the make on her and I'm tryin' to do somethin' serious.

Guys were walkin' around eating ice cream cones, hotdogs, you name it, and nobody cared.

The final payoff come one night in Montreal. I'm trying to do somethin' serious and some guy is walkin' around eatin' an ice-cream cone. I said, "That's it!"

Now, what I do is, I don't have a floor director. Poor MacLean has got to run everything through his ear, which is tough.

He doesn't know how much time is left—he can't see. The guy's not givin' him hand signals. They've got to give it to him through his earpiece.

What I'm doin', I'm talkin' and he's got to listen to the people in the truck. Well, this is pretty tough. That's distracting and I'm goin' on at ninety miles an hour.

I can tell when he's listening to the truck and not to me.

One night in Montreal, they were talkin' to him quite a lot and he couldn't be listenin' to me. The week before, somebody had cut the head off the statue of Sir John A. Macdonald.

So I know MacLean is not paying attention to me and I'm goin' on, "Can you imagine cuttin' off a good Kingston boy's head?"

Now he comes back and he had only heard the last bit and he says, "Well, folks, I'm sure you know what he's talking about is Sir John A. Macdonald."

I says, "Well, who did you think I was talkin' about—Kirk Muller?"

* * *

When I first started doing "Coach's Corner," they had two cameras. When the camera is on, the red light comes on. So they'd put the red light on one, and I'd start talkin'. Then they'd put the red light on over there. Then they'd go back to over here. Then they'd put the camera on Ron. They kept goin' back and forth.

For a year, I kept fightin' this, then I finally said, "I only want one camera."

They said, "There's nobody in television has one camera. Nobody. You have to have two."

I said, "I'm not havin' two. I can't be talkin', then all of a sudden, you're gonna put the light on over here. I want one camera."

This was after Hodge left and MacLean come. I used to do as I was told back in the Hodge days.

I said, "I want one camera and that's it, or I'm not doin' it."

What happened was, it worked out so much better. MacLean had to get so much closer to me, and people were tellin' me he was makin' faces and changin' expressions, and they were gettin' a bigger kick out of that than out of me sometimes.

That's why we're the only ones in television that only has one camera.

* * *

This was the very first time I did a show with Dan Kelly.

I asked Harry Sinden if I could go and do colour on a game with Dan Kelly on *Hockey Night in Canada* while I was coachin' the Bruins. He said I could, and they put that thing in my ear.

So while I was trying to answer the question Dan gave me — "Don, what do you think of Philadelphia?" or something — some guy was talking in my ear.

So I said, "I'll tell you, Dan, if this guy would quit talkin' in my ear."

AL'S NOTE: *Dan Kelly was one of the legendary* Hockey Night in Canada *announcers. He had a booming voice and an effervescent personality. In 1989, he won the Foster Hewitt Memorial Award as a tribute to his outstanding career. His son John has followed in his father's footsteps and does play-by-play for the St. Louis Blues.*

* * *

So then, when I started to do colour for serious and they had that thing in my ear, I'd just turn it down. I'd just start talkin' and they'd say "Commercial" and I'd stop.

So the producer come to me and said, "You've got to start finishin' your sentences."

I said, "But as soon as I hear 'Commercial,' I stop. I didn't go on any further once you said 'Commercial.'"

After a while, I just turned it off and they had to just work around me.

One time we had a new floor director. We didn't get to him to tell him not to count down. So he did it and he pointed. I said on television, "Yeah, I know what you're tellin' me. It's a television camera. You don't have to point at us."

* * *

I realize how tough it is to work with me, because we'll have it all planned a little bit. We sort of have an idea what we're gonna talk about, then all of a sudden, I'll get off on a tangent and I know for a fact they've got sponsors and everything and they want to go to commercials and they're yellin' at Ron, "Quit!" and I won't quit.

They're yellin' at him, "Quit! Quit! Get him off!"

How's he gonna stop me? It's live and I won't stop. And he gets blamed.

Unfortunately for him, when I go on something that I shouldn't have, he gets the blame, because they say, "You should have controlled him," and it happens all the time.

People think that it's easy to do stuff live, but it isn't.

One time in the playoffs, he got me mad about something and he kept going at me. We had three and a half minutes to go and I said, "I'm not speakin' anymore."

He said, "Well, no, we've still got time." And he says, "What about the water bottles?"

And I said, "No. I'm not speakin'. You ruined the story."

They're goin' nuts. What are they gonna do for three and a half minutes?

I says, "No, I'm not speakin'."

They didn't know what to do. And he kept arguing with me.

So they cut it short.

* * *

Bobby Schmautz walked in the dressing room one time. We were goin' into the playoffs and he hadn't scored in a while.

Harry was there and he walked in and said to me, in front of Harry, "Bench me. I'm not helpin' the club." That's the kind of guy he was. The club was the number one with him.

He made it very tough on me because Harry wasn't crazy about Schmautzie.

After, I says, "What are you doin', Schmautzie? Get out of here. As long as I'm here, you're gonna be playin'."

So we went into the playoffs and he scored eight goals on his first eight shots.

He was absolutely ruthless. When he didn't have a good scoring opportunity, he'd do what he called "waste one." He'd shoot it right at the goalie's head as hard as he could. He'd ring them off the mask, then the next one would be right along the ice. He was absolutely ruthless.

And scary. He was a scary guy, but I loved him.

* * *

We were a tough team in Boston. In fact, I'd have to say that some guys were vicious. But we'd have fun on the road.

Wayne Cashman said to me one time, "You know, every time my wife's driving me to the airport, I have a tough time not smiling."

New players would come in, and the players like Wayne Cashman and Bobby Schmautz would take them aside and say, "Look, we got something goin' here. We have a lot of fun on the road and we can do a lot of things. The one rule is, you never do anything in the hotel. You never embarrass Grapes. You never break a window or act up in the hotel. If he says to be in, be in. Don't screw it up!"

They didn't. They were more afraid of Cash and Schmautzie than me.

* * *

Our guys never acted up in the hotel. That was the rule.

One time we're in LA and at two in the morning, I get a call from a security guy. One of the guys won't get out of the pool.

I said, "Is he a little guy?"

He says, "Yeah."

I says, "Has he got a big nose?"

He says, "Yeah, come to think of it, he does have a big nose."

I said, "Well, you tell him I know who he is and he'd better be out of the pool in ten minutes or I'm comin' down."

That was the end of it.

AL'S NOTE: *The pool in question is in the Los Angeles Airport Marriott, the hotel that has been used by almost every NHL team during stays in Los Angeles ever since the Kings joined the league in 1967. The pool is outdoors and encircled by the hotel. Bobby Schmautz is only one of a long list of hockey players to be forcefully evicted from that pool after hours. And for that matter, a number of media members share that distinction as well.*

* * *

When I was in Boston, we were drivin' along a country lane near where we lived, and I saw this Corvette comin' about ninety miles an hour behind me.

Rose said, "Look at this maniac comin' along at ninety miles an hour!"

And this car roared past us on a country lane and then when it gets past us, the guy is hangin' out of the car sitting on the window frame, drivin' with one hand and wavin' back at us.

It was Schmautzie! He was Billy the Kid!

* * *

Him and Lanny McDonald, of all people, when I had them both in Colorado, formed a friendship you wouldn't believe.

Lanny wasn't like that, but he got like that when he was with Schmautzie.

They'd get out and go drinkin' and they'd both be slurring and you could hear Lanny all the time, "Everything in moderation, eh, Schmautzie?"

Then they'd laugh and Schmautzie would laugh and say, "Everything in moderation, Lanny."

* * *

Lanny and Schmautzie had this thing they would do when they were in line—like for customs at the airport. Lanny's mustache then was so big, you couldn't see his lips move.

So we'd be waiting for customs and Lanny would put his bag down in front of him. Schmautzie would kick the bag, and Lanny would go "Arf, arf," like there's a dog inside the bag. You couldn't see his lips.

This one time, Schmautzie kicked the bag and Lanny went "Arf, arf," and there was a little kid standing there with his mother watching and he started to cry because he thought there really was a dog in the bag.

All the people got upset and the police came. We had to open the bag to show them that there wasn't a dog, and the police were

Bobby wins again. Altogether between us we won Best Defenseman eight times, two scoring titles, MVP of playoffs, MVP of regular season, best ever plus versus minus +128, seven All-Stars, the Lester B. Pearson, MVP of the Canada Cup, two Stanley Cups, Coach of the Year.

Bobby at a prospect game in Calgary. He let me win the contest, does he ever get old?

Bobby at a charity game at St. Mike's arena when Ron was in danger of losing his job with the CBC.

I always liked that jacket.

Me telling Mr. Harper how to run the government after I was booed by the Bloc.

Frick and Frack during the 2008 Stanley Cup finals.

Ron telling the Terminator how to run California during the 2007 Stanley Cup final between Anaheim and Ottawa.

On the set of *Hockey Night in Canada* in 2002. We switched jackets as a joke, tried to look like each other. Best he's ever looked.

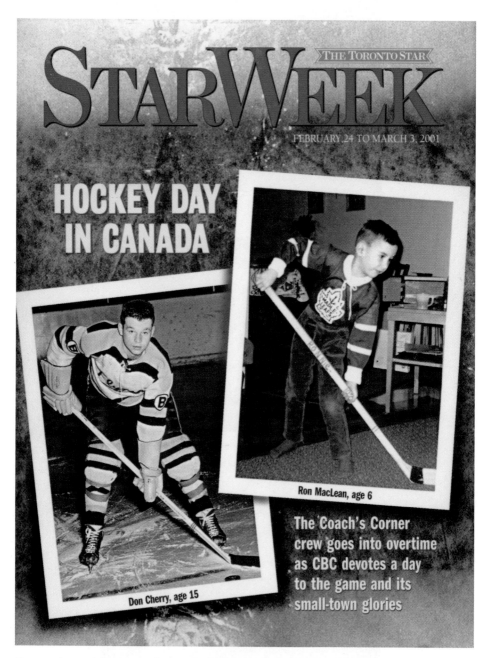

THE TORONTO STAR

STARWEEK

FEBRUARY 24 TO MARCH 3, 2001

HOCKEY DAY IN CANADA

Ron MacLean, age 6

Don Cherry, age 15

The Coach's Corner crew goes into overtime as CBC devotes a day to the game and its small-town glories

See people are right, now we know why he favours the Leafs, he's a closet Leaf from Red Deer, Alberta. Also note the inner tube rubber bands to hold my shin pads in place. Also note the new gloves my mother bought me when she saw the old gloves I was wearing. Mother's love.

Hockey Day in Canada in Winkler, Manitoba. My group dressed like me acting as escorts into the arena to do "Coach's Corner."

My buddy from Rochester, Whitey Smith, he rose from private to captain in combat in the Second World War, Whitey won the Bronze Star and other medals. I did not know this until after he died. He is pictured here on a balcony somewhere in Italy, we had great times together. He was my rock.

Fifth game in Detroit during 2008 Stanley Cup finals. Ron just asked the Kid if he was the guy who tripped Pittsburgh's goalie Fleury as he came on the ice for warm-up.

Ron Mac here telling Guy Lafleur how to play hockey and how to cut off the wing. Wayne saying, "Come on, I'm freezing." From left: Wayne Gretzky, me, Ron MacLean, Guy Lafleur.

Me and Corey Price. It is hard to believe that the kid did not get nominated for Rookie of the Year in 2008. He carried Montreal the last half of the season to first place.

Telling NBC and Gary and Brett Hull how to run the NHL.

Steve Livey, me, and Barry Melrose waiting for the red light for ESPN during the 2008 playoffs.

Me and the "Wounded Penguin" in Pittsburgh for Game 3 of the 2008 playoffs.

really ticked because they'd had to come all the way down and they looked foolish. They were going to take them away.

* * *

The very first time I coached in the old Chicago Stadium was 1974–75, my first year in the NHL, and in the first period, Bobby Orr and Stan Mikita got into some high-sticking and there was some bad feeling. There must have been bad feelings before.

It was an exhibition game, and I was surprised that they were high-sticking one another. After the game, Stan Mikita said, for some reason, "Cherry doesn't run that club. Bobby Orr runs that club."

I didn't know what to say about that. I was kinda stunned. I sorta collected my thoughts and Joe Giuliotti from the *Boston Herald-American* came to me about an hour later. He said, "Jeez, I missed the press conference. Can you give me a story? I gotta have a story."

I said, "Yeah, I'll give you a story. Bobby Orr and Stan Mikita got in a stick fight and for some reason, Mikita says that Cherry doesn't coach that club, Bobby Orr does. And I'm gonna tell you something. Stan Mikita has got a big mouth and somebody is going to send him back to Czechoslovakia in a pine box."

It made headlines in Boston and Chicago.

Well, the next day I'm back in Boston and I get a call from Mr. Campbell, the president of the league. I knew I was in deep trouble. When you get a call from Mr. Campbell, you're in deep trouble and you have to call him back.

I think his secretary's name was Diane, and she sounds like the voice of doom. She says, "I will tell Mr. Campbell you're on the line."

So he makes you wait three or four minutes, makes you sweat, then he answers the phone cold as ice like this: "Campbell here."

So sure enough, he says, "Explain your actions and your thoughts and what you said to the reporter in Chicago."

So I told him, and he says, "Do you realize what you have done? Do you realize that your future could be in jeopardy? If anybody on your team hurts Stan Mikita and they go to trial, *you* are in deep trouble. Do you understand? They could sue you and they could sue the Boston Bruins. Do you understand, young man?"

And I said meekly, "Yes, Mr. Campbell."

"And in the future, use your head for more than a hat rack."

* * *

Not long afterwards, in early 1975, came a game in Minnesota. It started out as just an average game. It was a rough game, but for us, that was an average game. And as I said before, we always had a tough time in Minnesota after Harry went on Minnesota television and said it was a shame that their players didn't play harder.

In this game, for some reason, Davie Forbes, who never had a history of violence—I don't even think I ever saw him in a fight before—had a fight with a guy by the name of Henry Boucha.

Henry Boucha was the guy who used to wear a bandana around his forehead. He looked pretty good.

So they had this fight, just an ordinary fight, and in Minnesota, they had the dumbest thing. They had the penalty boxes situated so that if you wanted to go to your bench, the two players would cross at centre ice.

That's exactly what happened. They get out of the box and they're yappin' all the way over, and at centre ice, Davie Forbes takes the butt end of his stick and drives it into Boucha's eye. I'm watchin' it, but I can't believe it!

I couldn't believe he would do that. I'd never seen him do anything like that before. Down goes Boucha, face down, blood's all over the ice. I can't believe it. Davie Forbes, I don't think he's never had a fight before, and here he does this.

He comes over to the bench and he's in a daze. I says, "You gotta go to the room." Naturally, he has been thrown out.

Well, about ten minutes later, the game is still on and Danny the trainer comes and says, "You'd better come to the room."

I says, "Why?"

He says, "You'd better come. I can't get Davie out of the shower. He's standing in there and he's got the water runnin' on him and it's like he's in a trance. He's just saying over and over, 'What have I done? What have I done? What have I done?'"

I go up to the dressing room. It was just behind the bench. I couldn't get him to come out of the shower. But finally, we got him out of the shower, and after that he was never the same. He was a changed guy. He became sort of a born-again Christian.

He actually changed for the better. He became quieter and nicer after that, but I guess you do when you have something like that happen to you.

They had the trial in Minny that summer. I had to fly out there. I really don't know how it got settled. There was some money given to Boucha.

But that was one of the most shocking things I ever saw. I had seen a lot worse, but it was shocking from a guy who had never had a fight before and never hurt anybody before do that.

Sometimes, when you get in a rage like that, it makes you do strange things.

* * *

Boucha was hurt bad and the whole thing ended up in court. To collect preliminary evidence, they came to the Boston Garden and they were questioning everybody—all the players, Harry and everybody.

So Harry says, "Now, don't act like a jerk when you get up there. And don't let them get you mad, 'cause that's what they want to do."

So they had me there and they're askin' me, "Mr. Cherry, your teams are noted for violence, and we saw you patting Forbes on the back as if you were saying, 'Well done.' Why did you do that?"

I said, "I wasn't patting him on the back saying, 'Well done.' I was patting him on the back saying, 'Don't worry about it. Don't worry about it.' I was consoling him."

So they said, "Also, in your history of violence, you said that you would send Mr. Mikita back to Czechoslovakia in a coffin."

I said, "No, I didn't."

"Oh yes, you did," they said, and they started to get out their books of newspaper clips and they took a long time pulling out their write-ups and their notes. And they say, "It's right here. This is what you said."

I said, "No. What I said was, we're goin' to send Stan Mikita back to Czechoslovakia in a pine box."

They were not amused.

AL'S NOTE: *The Forbes-Boucha incident occurred on January 4, 1975. Forbes was suspended for ten games by the NHL. He was later charged in criminal court and sued in civil court.*

The trial on the criminal charges resulted in a hung jury and the charges were dismissed. In the civil action, Boucha was awarded $1.5 million that was paid by Forbes, the Bruins and the NHL over an extended period.

* * *

Terry O'Reilly was a strange guy. He was one of the best fighters I've ever seen, but he wouldn't talk about fights. If a reporter asked him about a fight, he'd say, "I'd rather not talk about it. Let's talk about the hockey game." Unless you did something to him or his team mate he would not get involved in a fight, but once he got started, Katy, bar the door.

His hobbies were making stained-glass windows and collecting antiques. Him and I used to go around buying antiques, and I still have an antique aquarium that him and I got one day. I don't put fish in it. It has plants in it and stuff. But I've still got it in my basement. It's cast iron and it weighs a ton.

Terry was a strange guy. He had a violent temper, that's for sure. One thing is, you never crossed him.

He was a self-made man. When I played in Rochester, he was just a rookie. He played for the Boston Braves of the AHL, and he literally could not stand on his skates. He looked funny.

When he got to the Bruins, the guys gave him bob skates. He did not think it was funny. But he made himself into a hockey player, believe me. He could skate. He could score. But he had an awful temper.

We were in Atlanta one time and the Flames had an enormous big guy by the name of Harold Phillipoff. He was a giant. He didn't really want to fight Terry. He grabbed hold of Terry by both arms and he was swingin' him around. He made Terry look silly. We never said anything because it was Terry.

So the next time we're playing Atlanta, we're in Boston, and it was one of the hardest hits I've ever seen. Phillipoff is coming along, cutting across the blue line, and Terry is coming across the other way at a hundred miles an hour.

He hit him. It was like an explosion. The guy goes down on his back and he's flopping like a chicken on the ice.

They've got doctors on the ice, and I see Terry standing at the end of the bench, leaning on his stick. So I go down there. I figure I'd better go down there and console him. I said, "Terry, don't worry. I think he's gonna be all right. Don't worry."

Terry turned to me and he says, very quietly in a soft, calm voice, "Oh no Grapes, I really don't care if the ****er dies."

* * *

Terry was so fair all the time. He would never ever sucker a guy. He would tap people on the shoulder and say, "Let's go." He wanted to be honest and the whole deal.

I said "Terry, you're gonna get it one of these days. You're gonna tap somebody who's not as fair as you and he's going to sucker you."

But he kept doin' it all the time. He was a fair Irish lad.

One day, he tapped the wrong guy, Dan Maloney, another tough Irish lad, on the shoulder, and Dan just turned around and filled him right in. You should have seen his nose. We said nothin'. It would have been your life.

Well, Terry just stewed until the next time we played against Dan Maloney. When it happened, ooh, what a wipe-out job that was. No mercy. Terry could really throw 'em. And he was a left-hander too, which made it worse.

* * *

My dad sat me down when I went away from home to play junior hockey, he said, "There are going to be times when you play bad and you're going to be criticized, and it's going to hurt, and you're going to be down. There was a famous man who had a saying, it goes like this:"

"It is not the critic who counts; not the man who points out how the strong man stumbles, or where the doer of deeds could have done them better. The credit belongs to the man who is actually in the arena, whose face is marred by dust and sweat and blood; who strives valiantly; who errs, and comes short again and again, because there is no effort without error and shortcoming; but who does actually strive to do the deeds; who knows the great enthusiasms, the great devotions; who spends himself in a worthy cause; who at the best knows in the end the triumph of high achievement, and who at the worst, if he fails, at least fails while daring greatly, so that his place shall never be with those cold and timid souls who know neither victory nor defeat."

That was written by President Theodore Roosevelt.

* * *

I was out havin' a couple of pops with a buddy after the 2008 play-offs and he said, "The playoffs have been over for five days and you're still gettin' ripped in the paper for not giving Sidney Crosby credit on 'Coach's Corner' and praising Gary Roberts to the moon. Does it ever get you down?"

I had to admit when I first started on TV, it really did get me down. As I told you before, my first rip job was from a reporter I admired and he did a real hatchet job on me. It was a beauty. It threw me off so much I really didn't know if I could go back on TV.

But I bit the bullet and went back and did my best. And I found the longer I was on, and the more I got ripped, the thicker my hide got.

If you're going to give it out, you've got to be able to take it. As Harry Truman said, "If you can't take the heat, get out of the kitchen."

* * *

So my buddy said, "How did the disagreement with Crosby get started anyhow?"

It's a funny thing. I started it by trying to help Crosby. It started when he made a move on a young goalie in junior hockey. He put the puck in from behind the net after he'd scooped it up on his blade and shot it like he was using a lacrosse stick.

I have to admit it was a great move, but I felt sorry for the young goalie who had everybody laughing at him.

The move had been done before in college hockey, but that was in overtime. This time, it was done in a 4–0 game and there was no need for it. It was going to be a rout, so I said that he shouldn't have done that.

I also said that he should stop diving because when you get to the NHL, the refs get ticked off and they won't call anything when you're really fouled.

The people around him went nuts. The idea of criticizing a future star of hockey! They took it the wrong way.

But sure enough, he goes to the NHL and starts that stuff. The refs get ticked off and now they let anything go on him.

Proof? Think of the way he played in the playoffs—hell-bent for leather. Straight-ahead style. He only drew five penalties. Five penalties! Evgeni Malkin drew eleven. This is impossible. I showed it on "Coach's Corner" and people couldn't believe it.

The kid now has changed. No yapping at the refs. He plays it straight. But it's too late. He's got the tag.

And all I did was try to warn him.

* * *

As for Roberts, it does sound strange to praise a guy who only played ten minutes in a game and had no points, and not mention the guy who had two goals.

In the papers, they said it's not right for a high-profile commentator to make no effort to meet the future superstar of hockey.

Well, I never meet the players. I don't hang around teams. I don't hang around benches and dressing rooms. I never met Vincent Lecavalier, either, and I praised him to the hilt.

I met a few guys in Toronto because until last year, our *Hockey Night in Canada* studio was right next to the Maple Leafs' dressing room.

I don't go out for dinner with players or try to get chummy with them. That's not my style.

That night they were talkin' about, I knew that Crosby, with his two goals, would be praised to the moon by our guys who are doing the game.

I try to point out the insider stuff. When Maxime Talbot scored the tying goal in the last minute and everyone was jumping around for joy, Roberts was checking the clock, and that's what I showed on "Coach's Corner." We also showed him on the bench pumping up Talbot right before the tying goal and Talbot nodding his head, then going out and scoring.

That's what I love.

But I was criticized on radio and TV and especially in the papers for concentrating on Roberts and not Crosby.

The day I got back from the playoffs, I got a call from Steve

Ludzik, who said, "Grapes, I loved it when you showed Roberts looking at the clock."

Ludzik played in the National Hockey League and he coached in the National Hockey League and that's good enough for me.

* * *

Michel Therrien had benched Roberts for the first game. He didn't want to break up a winning lineup, he said.

Roberts was seething. He didn't speak to the press about it that day. When he finally did talk, they said, "Why aren't you playing?" and he said, "Ask the coach."

I was listening to Nick Kypreos on a radio show in Toronto and he was on with two guys who were really criticizing Roberts for criticizing the coach. They said it was wrong. "Look at Hasek. Look at Chelios. They never played and they never complained."

Nick said, "Wait a minute! Are you two guys crazy? We're talkin' about Gary Roberts here, the heart and soul of the team. Chelios hardly ever played at all in the playoffs. He was the seventh defenceman. And Hasek never played after the first round. You're comparing that?" Of course Roberts should have complained. He should have been in the first game!

* * *

What I try to do is show what goes on at the bench. Steve Ludzik, he's a coach. He knew what was goin' on at the bench. Nick Kypreos, he played like Roberts, a heart-and-soul guy, he knew what was goin' on at the bench.

That's what I try to do. Maybe I do try to please guys like this too much, but that's my style and I'm not going to change now.

I do get carried away sometimes with guys, especially Bobby Orr. Why shouldn't I? He's the greatest hockey player who ever played. And when I see Bobby flying through the air after scoring the winning goal in the Stanley Cup finals against Glenn Hall and the St. Louis Blues — and I've seen it over a hundred times — I still get chills.

And when I play that segment with Bobby that my son, Tim, made with all Bobby's goals and the song in the background, "Nobody Does it Better" by Carly Simon, I get all teary-eyed, thinkin' of Bobby and that he had to quit at 28.

When I see Roberts pumping up Talbot on the bench with two minutes to go and Talbot comes through, I get excited and forget about everything else. I suppose that's not good television and it's wrong, but that's the way that I feel.

So I said to my friend, "Does that answer your question?"

He said, "Not really. It's okay to praise Roberts but you shouldn't ignore guys like Crosby who scored two goals. You had to be reminded on ESPN by Barry Melrose that the kid scored two goals."

I had no answer because he's right, of course. But when I come home and I hear guys like Steve and Nick, I know I've done the right thing.

* * *

Terry O'Reilly, who was a very, very intense hockey player, came to me one day and he says, "You know, there's absolutely no sense at all shooting at Gerry Cheevers in practice because he makes no attempt to stop the puck. It ruins every practice."

So I call a meeting for the players without the goalies. I said, "I'll tell you what. Let's try it this way. If you hit Gerry on the right pad, we'll count that as a goal, because he's good at getting out of the way."

Well, nobody ever told Gerry — naturally. So practices went on and scrimmages went on and Gerry came to me and he says, "Grapes, have you noticed how good I'm playing in practices?"

I said, "Oh yeah, Gerry, you're doin' a great job."

But unfortunately for me, somebody told him what was goin' on. He didn't talk to me for a week.

* * *

When I was in Colorado, we had a great bunch of guys. It's too bad we had a general manager, Ray Miron, who, I felt, disliked us so intensely. All we needed was a goaltender.

It really hurt. We had Dougie Favell, a good little goaltender, living right in Colorado up in the mountains. He was not playin' at all. He could have helped us and he had played for Colorado before. The GM wouldn't talk to him because Dougie had said somethin' to him when he left.

It's too bad. We had great guys. We had Walter McKechnie. We had Lanny McDonald. Rene Robert. Bobby Schmautz. Mike Christie. Ronnie Delorme. I could go down the list.

We had the makings of a real great club. The crowds were comin' back. In our last game of the year, we had 13,000 in the worst snowstorm of the year. We could have had a complete sellout.

It was just so sad. We had great team spirit, too. We were always together. We were near the end, I think it was our second-last game, and Kevin Morrison, a big guy from Sydney, Nova Scotia, kept saying that the guys from the east, the Maritimers, were better drinkers than the guys from the west.

Lanny was givin' him a hard time 'cause he was from Hanna, Alberta.

So they came up with the idea of having a drinking contest, McDonald from the west against Morrison from the Maritimes.

We had two days to go before a road game in Winnipeg, so they set it all up. It was eight o'clock at night. We had the beer on ice. We made the bets. I think there was about $300 riding on it.

So Lanny and Kevin started drinkin'. You didn't have to take it down fast. You had a couple of minutes to drink the beer. So we got goin' and Kevin is pullin' ahead. I was sort of cheering for Kevin 'cause he was from the east.

But I never dreamed that a little skinny guy like Lanny could keep up with Kevin Morrison, who was noted for having a few.

So they had two. No problem. Three. No problem. Four. They're goin' along. Five. Six. Seven. Eight. Nine.

Now I can see Kevin is startin' to waver a little bit. Lanny, he's just like it doesn't matter at all.

I think they got up to eighteen beers and it was coming out Kevin's nose and he cried uncle.

Bobby Schmautz was like Lanny's trainer, helping him along. He had a towel waving and everything, like in a boxing ring.

Kevin quit at his eighteenth. Lanny twisted around, twirled his moustache and said, "Schmautzie, crack me another one, will ya please?" Ya can't beat those Western guys.

* * *

Every guy on the team was at the drinking contest except one— Mike McEwen. It figured.

We had a great young defenceman with us at the time. His name was Barry Beck. He was very upset that we had a first-round draft choice who was a floater and was sent down to Fort Worth, but was makin' a lot more money than him.

He was very dissatisfied. He played good for us, but I could understand the way he felt. At the time, I'd say he was one of the top five or ten defencemen in the league. He had a shot like a rocket—and heavy. He was big guy and tough, and here he is, earning half the money of a floater in Fort Worth.

So management came to me and I said, "Well, you should give him what he's worth."

But they wouldn't give him what he was worth, so we traded him to the New York Rangers, who gave us next to nothing in return. They gave us Mike McEwen, who I knew I would not get along with.

It was not fun from the very first day. For some reason, Armand Pohan and Arthur Imperatore were in love with him. Imperatore was the owner, and Pohan was his stepson.

They loved McEwen because they lived in New Jersey and they saw him when he was playing with the New York Rangers. He had twenty goals one year as a defenceman, which is pretty good, but he was not doing the job here, and he would stay on the ice. As long as the play was going, he'd stay on. And I like short shifts.

So him and I were down to the nitty-gritty. He wasn't a very big guy, and when he stayed on, he'd get tired and he'd cost us goals.

So we had a long talk: "Now listen, come off the ice after forty-five seconds—no more than a minute."

He'd stay out too long—two minutes sometimes—get tired, cough up the puck and give up the winning goal.

I says, "I'm warning you! Don't do it again."

So sure enough, the next game, we're winning 3–2, playing the Islanders. What does he do? He stays out for two minutes, coughs up the puck. Tie game.

He came to the bench. I grabbed him by the front of the sweater, lifted him up off the bench and nailed him against the glass.

Unfortunately for me, it was on *Hockey Night in Canada*. I knew my days were numbered when I did that because he was a friend of the owners.

He quit the team and he must have gone to New Jersey and the owners must have said, "Listen, don't worry about it. You come back and we'll get rid of Cherry at the end of the season."

That's what happened.

AL'S NOTE: *The Barry Beck trade to the Rangers was considered to be something of a blockbuster at the time. It occurred on November 9, 1979, and in return for Beck, Colorado got McEwen, Pat Hickey, Lucien DeBlois, Dean Turner and Bobby Crawford. It sounds like a lot, but in reality, Don is dead right when he says the Rockies got "next to nothing" in return.*

* * *

My experiences with Mike McEwen were not good. I could go on and say more, but what's the point?

I'll just say that after he left Colorado, he was playing with the New York Islanders one night and I was doing the game for *Hockey Night in Canada* with Danny Gallivan.

We were way up high, doing the game. The TV booth was in the last row of the Nassau County Coliseum, so we were way up high and this woman kept turning around and hollering at me.

I finally recognized her. It was Mike McEwen's wife.

She kept hollering at me. I said, "Hey, I see Mike is still putting you up in the cheap seats."

* * *

Wilf Paiement was from northern Quebec, and his father was a great hunter. He gave me a set of moose antlers which I still have at my cottage.

Two days later, we traded him. He was very upset. We traded him to Toronto for Lanny McDonald.

A lot of fans think that was a bad trade for Toronto because they liked Lanny and he was a character guy, but if you look at the records, Wilf was the highest-scoring right winger Toronto ever had until Ricky Vaive came along.

He did well, but he was very upset when it happened. He said, "They won't like me in Toronto because I'm French-Canadian."

That's the way they think, but he could pump in the goals like you wouldn't believe. Good guy.

Wilf had a tough time with a guy by the name of Dennis Polonich.

Dennis Polonich was one of those pests that was always stickin' guys. He used to do that to Brad Park, and Park used to fight with him, and when he did, Polonich had done his job—Brad Park was off for five minutes.

I said, "Look, Brad, you leave him alone. Don't worry about him. Don't even look at him. We'll have somebody take care of him. Don't worry."

But Polonich kept givin' it to Wilf, and Wilf carved him up pretty good. Boy, did he get him in the face with his stick! He was a stick man. He had no mercy, Wilf, if you bugged him.

They had a lawsuit, and I guess Polonich made a lot of money, but it didn't make any difference to Wilf. No matter who you were, big or small, he had those wacko eyes. A good guy and a good hockey player.

AL'S NOTE: *The incident happened on October 25, 1978. Polonich suffered a broken nose, a concussion and a number of cuts. Paiement was suspended for fifteen games. In 1982, Polonich was awarded a settlement of $850,000.*

* * *

Hazing was a part of hockey. In a different form, it still is now. They make the rookies go out and buy expensive dinners.

But back a few years, it was a lot different. When I first went to the Bruins, they tied up three guys, put mops on them and did a few other things. To me, it was degrading. They had cans of spaghetti that they put in a bucket and put the guys' feet in it. They told them it was worms.

I stopped it after my first year. It's ridiculous, as far as I'm concerned. I never liked it. I know a lot of people like it, but I was against it even before the left-wing tree-huggers were against it.

The funny thing is, they never did it to the tough guys. They only did it against somebody else. But I've seen them get little guys, pull them down and shave the front of their heads.

One guy, they held him down—and he was an obnoxious little so-and-so, so I was kinda glad to see them do it—and the only thing he had goin' for him was the front of his head. He had lovely, beautiful hair. And they shaved half of it off. The guys called him Sky Low Low after that.

You know what he was goin' to do? He was goin' to charge them with assault, and the team had to stop him.

I never really believed in it. You don't want guys grabbin' guys and holdin' them down and shavin' them in certain areas. You know where I mean. It really is degrading, but everybody did it, so when I was younger, I just stood there and watched.

One time I thought it was really funny. There was one guy in juniors who was always the one shavin' the guy. I said, "Jeez, I notice that you're always the one holdin' the guy's you-know-what. When you're shavin', you seem to enjoy it."

He said, "What? What are you saying?"

I said, "Well, I don't know. You seem to always be the one who's holding it while a guy's gettin' shaved. It looks like you're enjoyin' it."

Well, the guy went nuts.

The very first time it happened in Colorado, Armand Pohan and Arthur Imperatore were there. They didn't understand that stuff. They come to see our practice, and here the guys have some guy down and they're shavin' him.

No wonder they sold the team.

* * *

In my first year in junior hockey, there was a guy who was a wise-guy rookie. They always get the wise guys. I was a rookie too, and the guys were goin' around sayin' that a guy on the team could lift three guys.

I'm listenin' and kinda thinkin', "How could a guy lift three guys?"

They're sayin', "Oh yeah, he can do it."

This is goin' on and everybody is layin' bets and I'm kinda interested too. This wise-guy rookie with me is yappin' away—"Aw, you can't lift three guys."

So after practice they said, "Well, look, here's what we have to do. We have to have a guy in the middle, layin' on the floor. We have to put another guy behind him and he puts his arms around the guy's chest just under his arms. Then the third guy sits facing them and they have to entwine their legs around his middle. Then the guy who's going to lift will pick up the middle guy, and the other two will be hangin' on, so he'll pick up all three."

So this wise-guy rookie is layin' bets and he's gonna be the one in the middle. So when they get it all set up, they say to the guy on one end, "Can you move?"

"No, I can't move."

They say to the guy on the other end, "Can you move?"

"No, I can't move."

Then they said to the rookie in the middle, "Can you move?"

"No, I can't move."

"Okay, bring in the shaving stuff."

* * *

We lost Bob "Battleship" Kelly to the St. Louis Blues in my second year coaching Rochester. I had to find another tough guy because I had to have the toughest guy and the toughest team.

I didn't know where I was going to get another Battleship Kelly. Somebody told me about a fellow from Maxville, Ontario, who played for Cornwall. The word was that Cornwall won the Memorial Cup because they had a guy who terrorized the other team.

That was John Wensink. I wondered how he looked, because to be tough like that, you have to look tough. So I was goin' to the Hockey Hall of Fame—this was when it was at the CNE grounds—and I knew there would be a picture of the Memorial Cup champions.

I saw the picture, and wow! Boy, did he look tough! They called him "Wire" because he had wiry hair—and you couldn't believe how much there was of it because that was the style back then.

And he had a Fu Manchu mustache and he was six foot two. Did he look tough!

St. Louis had drafted him. I phoned the St. Louis Blues' general manager and I said, "If this guy doesn't make your club, I'd be interested in havin' him."

He said, "All right. I'll keep you in mind."

So when training camp come, I phoned him and I said, "Is he gonna make your club?"

He says, "Make our club? He can't even make our American league club. We're gonna send him down to Port Huron."

I says, "No, no. I'll take him."

He says, "Don, you don't want this guy. He can't even skate. There's no way you want him."

I says, "I'll take him."

He says, "No, you're gonna get mad at me once you see him. I don't want to do it."

I says, "Look, I will take him sight unseen. I want him."

He says, "All right. It's your funeral."

* * *

So they flew him to Rochester. I met him off the plane. You should have seen the size of him. He was more scary than Battleship Kelly. Big neck, big arms, a big farm boy.

I looked at his skates. They were fallin' apart. The Blues wouldn't even give him new skates. They thought he couldn't even make Port Huron.

So I got him and I was thrilled. He couldn't skate very good, I must admit. So he was my project, and I heard what he had done in Cornwall. He had scared half the other teams just by looking at them. He was a big part of their club because he also nailed a few guys, believe me.

So I got him and I worked with him on his skating. I said, "Look, John, don't forget: don't be afraid to fall down. What you're doin' is playin' it safe. You're gonna turn sharp, it doesn't matter if you fall down. You've got to get goin'."

So while we were there, he did improve.

* * *

There are a lot of stories I could tell about John, and maybe I will. But in the meantime, there's one story I like. He had hurt his knee and we're going down to Jacksonville, and if we win that game, we had first place clinched for the whole league.

So we're going down there and our PR man, John Den Hammer, said, "Look, it's around Christmas. Why don't you go home to see your parents? You can't play anyhow. I won't tell Don. You go home and you'll be back before they come off the road trip."

Well, I get down in Florida, and it's beautiful weather and I thought, "You know, I should have John Wensink come down here and enjoy the sun. That's not fair, him up in Rochester in the cold and the rest of us down here."

So I phoned John Den Hammer and I said, "Send down Wensink."

He says, "Well, no, I don't think it's a good idea."

I said, "I don't care that you don't think it's a good idea. Send him down."

Now Den Hammer has to get him back from Maxville, Ontario, and send him down.

In the meantime, we're playing in Jacksonville that night and John Hanna was the player-coach of the other team and it was for first place overall. We were short, so I just picked a name and I just put in John Wensink, just to have a name in the lineup.

I knew he couldn't play and the other team knew he couldn't play. They knew he wasn't there and they were bangin' us pretty good.

But at the end of the first period, I noticed John had arrived and he was standing there watching the game. We had his equipment there, so I said, "John, put on your equipment."

He said, "Grapes, I can't play."

I said, "I don't care. Put on your equipment."

So he puts on the equipment and when we go back out for the second period, he goes out. He can just skate a little and he goes to the bench and he stands at the end of the bench.

So John Hanna goes nuts. He's screaming, "You can't do that. You can't just bring in guys who weren't here and put them in the lineup!"

So they went and got the lineup sheet and sure enough, there's his name.

So Wensink just stood there and acted as if he was going to go over the boards every time one of those guys looked as if they were going to smack us around like they did in the first period.

He'd look at me, as if he wanted permission to go over, and the other team was terrified. I'd say, "No, no, John. Stay back. Not yet."

We kept pumpin' in the goals. They wouldn't even look at us sideways after John showed up. It was the only time a hockey player ever won a game for his team just by standing on the bench.

We won first place overall, and after the game we went to a place called Someplace Else.

I was sitting there like a king. Bobby Ellett got me a big tray of cheese and we're sittin' there drinkin', singin' songs, havin' fun. First place overall.

It doesn't get any better. First place, having a few pops with the guys. We were like a band of pirates, an independent club in the days of the WHA that took everybody. It was unbelievably great. Moments to live forever.

* * *

We were in Providence playing the Reds and a beautiful guy by the name of Bert Wilson was looking for trouble.

It was the first time I ever said anything like this. And the last time.

I said to John, "John, would you like to take a shift against this guy?"

That's all I said. He said, "I think I would, Grapes."

So I put him on against Bert. Well, you never saw such a fight! They called it World War III. Everybody that was on the ice joined in. The bodies were piled up behind. There was blood on the glass. In the *New York Daily News*, it took the whole back page and they showed the bodies piled up in the fight.

One guy was carried off with a broken leg.

The state troopers came in with their jackboots and their sunglasses and their big helmets to get me and their players.

John Muckler was the coach on the other side. He come on the ice and he was trying to get at me. I was gonna go, too, and I thought, "I've got a brand new suit, but I'll go anyhow."

But then he realized what he had done, so he went back.

I was waving to one of the owners up in the press box to come and help, but he said, "No way."

It was the battle of battles. The referee had to take a long time to hand out all the penalties, and I wanted to see a copy of the report he wrote to the league after the game because I knew we were going to get suspensions, but I wanted to see what he wrote that night.

I knew the guys were dyin' of thirst, so I said, "Look, get on the bus. Go ahead and go to that bar down the street and I'll be there in a while."

I had to sit and wait and wait and wait. And I finally got the referee's report. I go out and there's the bus still sittin' there.

Bobby Ellett, captain of the team said, "If you couldn't come over and have a pop with us and you had to wait, we were waitin' too."

I knew they were dry as a desert, but that's true love.

* * *

The upshot was that the owner of the Providence Reds tried to get John Wensink suspended, and he did. He got ten games.

But they didn't know that John had hurt his knee and he couldn't play anyhow.

Well, it just happened that when his suspension expired, the next game was against the Providence Reds in Providence.

Well, they played it up. There was gonna be World War IV.

Wilson is waitin' for him. We're gonna do this. We're gonna do that. They were lookin' for a sellout.

So I phoned Ed Duckworth. He was the writer for the Providence paper. I said, "Seeing as they hate John Wensink so much, I am not bringin' him, so John Wensink will not be in our lineup when we come to Providence."

The Providence owner went crazy! He went to the league and said, "Cherry cost me $50,000 saying that."

Unbeknownst to them, John couldn't come because he still had a bad knee. Lovely.

* * *

While we were at that game, the trainer came to me and said, "There's a guy outside and he says he's a hockey player. He says if he can have the warmup with us the next time we're back in Providence, he'll give us $500."

I thought, "Hey, $500. Not bad. I can give it to the guys for a party. In the warmup, how bad can the guy be?"

So I said, "Okay, next time in."

Well, it just so happened that this was the time that Wensink did come back for real. Jack Butterfield, the president of the league, is there to make sure nothing happens. Everybody is there and the guy came with his $500 and his bag.

I said, "Jeez, how about doin' it the next time? This is a touchy situation."

He says, "Mr. Cherry, I have all my friends here. Everybody's here. I've made bets with everyone. I have to go on."

So I think, "Well, how bad can the guy be? We'll put him in one of our sweaters and he'll just take some shots."

He goes out for the warmup and the trainer comes runnin' in and says, "Grapes, he can't even stand up on his skates!"

So I go out to see this guy in warmup and the trainer is right. He's teetering around, hangin' on to the boards.

I know I'm for it 'cause Jack Butterfield has got to see this kid doin' this. Sure enough, I get a letter and he's ticked to no end — I'm making a mockery of the game, the kid could have got hurt, etc., etc.

So I write back and try to back out by saying I did it to try to bring fans into the building. I say that the guy brought fifty friends and that I'm donating the money he gave to charity.

I don't think Jack Butterfield bought it, but he did let me off the hook.

The worst part, though, was that the kid had promised us $500 but only came through with $250. It made for a smaller party.

* * *

A couple of years ago, I was asked by the Pittsburgh Penguins if I'd do their television for them. I had already done something — some little skit for them or somethin' in between periods — and I thought as a joke, I'd say I'd do something for them.

So I went down and they were really gonna do stuff for me — send a jet for me, fly me down, have me do a game, fly me back, pay me pretty good dough — but I really wasn't interested. I just wanted to do *Hockey Night in Canada*.

So I get down there and I'm doin' an interview between the first and second periods, and Jagr had got hurt and he'd laid on the ice — you know, one of those deals — and that's when he had long hair.

So the guy is interviewing me and I said, "Yeah, you got a tough decision to make when Yammy lays on the ice. You don't whether to send out for his hairdresser or his jeweller."

They weren't too happy.

AL'S NOTE: *Don isn't big on the pronunciation of certain names, and "Jaromir" falls into that category. He calls him "Yammy."*

* * *

To make it worse, between the second and third periods, they were showing a picture from the program, and for some reason, it had a picture of Yammy and Mario Lemieux standing back to back with their shirts off.

At that time, they both had long hair. You can imagine what I said.

I said, "There's Mario and his daughter." That didn't go over too good. Evidently, Jagr's agent went to the Pittsburgh people and said, "If you hire Cherry, Yammy's gonna quit." Or something like that.

I wasn't going to do it anyhow. But that was the end of my time with the Pittsburgh Penguins.

* * *

At that time, too, I was running out of places to go. With the Calgary Flames, I'd go and do a thing sort of like *Hockey Night in Canada* — well, it was *Hockey Night in Canada*, but it was for the Calgary Flames.

It was in Boston, and the Flames had a guy called Pekka Rautakallio. I started right off the bat. I said, "It's tough to say 'Pekka' in Boston. You have to think about that."

That didn't go over with the producer too good.

Calgary gets up 3–0 and they were doing real good, but I could see that Stan Jonathan was pickin' on Pekka Rautakallio. I said, "Look, you gotta get Randy Holt out there to play for Pekka Rautakallio because Stan Jonathan is after him."

Randy Holt could at least hold his own against Jonathan anyhow. Randy Holt was afraid of no one.

So sure enough, Pekka Rautakallio throws it away when Jonathan comes at him and the Bruins have their first goal. Now it's 3–1.

Second goal, he throws the puck away again. Won't go in the corner with Jonathan. Now it's 3–2.

And believe it or not, Rautakallio was on the ice when Jonathan scored a goal. He wouldn't check him.

I said, "They've got to get that Pekka Rautakallio off the ice when Jonathan is around. He's as yellow as a duck's foot."

Cliff Fletcher was the general manager for the Flames then, and I guess Pekka Rautakallio's wife was phonin' him and cryin'. That was my last time ever doin' colour for the Calgary Flames.

* * *

Now I'm doin' colour for *Hockey Night in Canada*, being loaned out. It was sort of like a Harry Neale job, or I guess Greg Millen now. That's what I used to do.

I'm doin' a game in Winnipeg, and I won't mention the guy's name on the Jets because it's sort of embarrassing. Anyhow, he had got married and on the honeymoon, the wife had fallen in love with the lifeguard.

They came back to Winnipeg after the honeymoon, and she turned right around and went right back down south. He must have been a pretty good lifeguard.

So this guy for months was playin' lousy, but everybody loved him in Winnipeg. He really was a nice guy.

But for months he's playin' lousy. How long can you go?

I was doin' the colour, I forget the announcer. It might have been Don Wittman.

So this guy's still playing lousy and the other colour guy says, "Well, he has an excuse. He has personal problems."

I says, "Personal problems? Get out there and play! What's he doin'? We all have personal problems. He's a professional. He's paid to play and he's just goin' through the motions because he's got personal problems? Buck up! Be a professional! Be a trooper! Get out there and play."

And I proceeded to rip him pretty good.

Well, in the morning I got on one of those little shuttle buses to go to the airport. It was about six in the morning and they had the local radio on. You should have heard one of those mornin' sports guys give it to me.

He called me an insensitive barbarian, et cetera, et cetera.

I never got invited back to do any more games in Winnipeg.

*　*　*

Now I'm runnin' out of teams. I'm goin' all over, doin' colour, and I'm goin' down to Montreal. I was told not to be cheerin' so much for the Boston Bruins, and Montreal is playin' Boston.

So the score is 3–3 and I'm doin' pretty good, not favourin' the Bruins too much. It was late in the game, and Craig MacTavish spun around and put the puck in the top corner and the Bruins go on top 4–3.

When he put that puck in, I said, "We're beatin' those Canadiens tonight. We're beatin' those Canadiens tonight."

It was the last time I ever did colour for the Montreal Canadiens.

*　*　*

Now I'm doin' colour for the Vancouver Canucks.

Pavel Bure, who I really liked later and got to know—and he liked me, I don't know why—was playin' for Vancouver.

Like I say, I liked him, but he was a dirty little guy. Remember the time he elbowed Shane Churla in the head? That was a great elbow. Gordie Howe would have been proud of it.

Anyhow, at the time I was doin' the game, it's a game with Boston Bruins again and he slew-footed Cam Neely. I showed it and I said, "Look at this little weasel—slew-footing Cam Neely! This guy is a weasel."

Well, I got it in the paper the next day and from then on it was "Weasel Power"—they had signs saying "Weasel Power" and everything.

That was the last time I ever did colour for the Vancouver Canucks.

AL'S NOTE: *Bure delivered a vicious elbow to the head of Shane Churla in the second round of the 1994 playoffs. Churla was playing for the Dallas Stars at the time and went down as if he had been poleaxed. Astonishingly, no suspension was handed down by Brian Burke, who was in charge of NHL discipline at the time.*

Had the Canucks been deprived of Bure's services, they might not have made their subsequent run to the Stanley Cup final against the New York Rangers. On the other hand, Churla did not miss a game—but that was the era before the advent of today's strict rules regarding players who suffer concussions.

* * *

One time, this was before Ron and I stopped goin' in bars, we were in a bar after a game, and Pavel Bure's father was in there.

We were sittin there and this drink came over. I said, "Where's this from?"

They said, "Pavel's father sent it over."

I said, "Check it, will you, please?" This was after I'd called Pavel a weasel.

But Pavel and I became good friends. We were on the set in Montreal one night and he came in to say hello.

Of course, he had five guys with him wearing long black leather coats. He always had those guys around him. But him and I got along. It was strange.

* * *

There was a young—how would I call the guy?—a young crackerjack boss, or so he thought, with *Hockey Night in Canada*. He didn't understand me at all.

I think he went out to Hollywood after this. He used to make the road trips in jeans and a T-shirt. You know, one of those guys. Running shoes and all that.

On this trip, we're doin' Edmonton and LA. They've been buildin' up the return of Gretzky to Edmonton. It must have been 1988. The return of Gretzky to Edmonton, one of the greatest things of all time. They're goin' on and on. It was absolutely sickening to listen to.

So, at the end of the first period, I said, "You know, seein' Gretzky wearing that LA uniform is like seein' Secretariat at a state fair."

Well, this producer went insane. He never said anything to me. He said it to Ronnie Harrison, the director.

He said, "What are we doin'? What are we havin' this guy on for? Here we come out and we spend all this money and he's puttin' it down. I don't understand it."

He never said anythin' to me, but somehow it got back to me.

Now, I do have a death wish. So the next morning, they're sittin' having breakfast at the hotel, and I go over and start to antagonize him.

So now we get on the plane and I open up the *Edmonton Sun*. I don't know the writer's name. I wish I did. Someday I'm goin' to find out the writer's name and bless him. Bless him, that's all I can say.

It had a great big headline: "Vintage Grapes saves CBC." And it was a write-up about how it'd been a nothing broadcast, but I was great. I'm gonna find out this guy's name some time and send him a letter and thank him.

So I ripped it out, and this boss is sittin' up front with one of his flunkies, and I slammed it right down in front of him.

And I said to him, "*This* goes on all the time and *this* is why I'm the best guy you've ever had."

Now he's really ticked.

Ronnie Harrison, he's a good guy and I love him, I tell ya, but I was really ticked at him that day too. He's sittin' over beside me, and I'm givin' it to him all the way to Toronto.

He's pretending he's workin', but I won't stop—"Ronnie, you used to be a good guy," and so on. Now I have the executive producer, the director and the producer all ticked at me, but I'll tell you one thing: when I opened that paper and I saw "Vintage Grapes saves CBC," it was another one of those moments to live forever.

But I do really think that sometimes I have a death wish.

* * *

One time, when Gerry McNamara was general manager, the Toronto Maple Leafs smuggled this player, Miroslav Ihnacak, out of Czechoslovakia. They even gave him Number 27. They gave him Frank Mahovlich's number! He was supposed to be the saviour of saviours, this guy.

Ballard was in the paper, talkin' about how great this guy was and how lucky they were to smuggle him out. "We're so glad we've got him," he's sayin', and stuff like that.

I see the first period, and this guy is brutal. I tell ya, he's a little guy. He's nothing, just nothin'.

Frank Mahovlich? Are you kidding?

So I get on TV and I says: "Listen, I'll tell you one thing. This guy Ihnacak is not a hockey player. This is not the guy. What happened was, McNamara was driving along the highway in Czechoslovakia and picked this guy up. This guy is a plumber. This guy will never play in the National Hockey League. In fact, this guy will never play in the American Hockey League. He's brutal."

So now this producer comes on and he's whinin', "What did you have to say that for?"

We're in the little green room and the call comes through: "Ballard wants you to call him right now."

Now the producer starts again. "See what you've done? See what you've done? You've cost me my career."

I said, "Who cares about your career? If I'm done, I'm done."

Now he says, "You're always thinkin' about yourself. What about me?"

So he tried to get through to Ballard and he couldn't get through. He's sitting there whining and his stomach is in knots. Finally, he gets through and Ballard says, "Listen, Wendel Clark's grandmother is in the crowd. Get a shot of her, will ya?"

AL'S NOTE: *In an attempt to save face, the Leafs kept putting Miro Ihnacak into the lineup, even though he didn't deserve to be there. Then they shipped him to Detroit, one of the few teams that was as bad as the Leafs. Even so, Ihnacak managed to dress for only fifty-six NHL games.*

* * *

Another time, I had to tape "Coach's Corner" and I say that Mike Vernon, at the time, is the greatest goalie playin' today. I go on and on. Vernon had been playin' well and I say, "There's nobody like Mike Vernon."

So the first period starts, and the first four shots on Mike Vernon, he lets in.

It's 4–0 and they pull Vernon, so I go to the producer, the guy that was whinin' in the room, and I say, "You can't play this, because I say he's great and he just let in four goals."

He says, "Oh, you're always worried about something."

I said, "YOU CAN'T PLAY IT!"

He says, "Oh, you worry too much. It doesn't matter."

I said, "I come on and say he's the greatest goalie in the game and he's down 4–0. It doesn't matter?"

But he won't change his mind.

So I say, "Okay, that's it. I'm leavin' and I'm never comin' back."

So I was out. I was gone.

I get halfway out and Rick Scully, who I was partners with in the restaurants, caught up to me and he says, "Don, you've got to go back."

So I go back and it was the first time they'd ever done it. They sent out "Coach's Corner" live by satellite as I was doin' it. They cancelled the other one. They found out they could do it that way, and from then on, most of them were live.

But I've never forgotten that producer. He didn't care one way or another that I would have looked like the biggest fool of all time.

Which a lot of people say I am.

* * *

During the lockout, they were showin' some of the classic games and they were showing the one from the 1980 playoffs when I had too many men on the ice.

It was a great game, I have to admit that.

While they were doin' it, they were choppin' bits of it and cuttin' it down. I was waitin' in a room off the studio because I was supposed to comment on it when it was over.

They were ruinin' the whole thing, so I came out of the room just steamin'. "What is goin' on here?" I'm just goin' nuts.

We're in the studio and everybody is there. There's got to be about fifty or sixty guys and the head guy says, "If you've got anything to say, say it to me."

I says, "Who the **** do you think I'm sayin' it to?"

And he says, "We'll go outside and talk about it."

I says, "We'll go outside all right," and I grabbed my coat and I go home.

So I get home and Rose is sittin' in the corner, kinda lookin' at the TV. She always read a magazine while the game was goin' on. So she thinks I'm comin' on at the end of the first.

I come in steamin', throwin' my coat down, and sit down.

She never says a word. Then she looks up and says, "Aren't you supposed to be on at the end of the period?"

I says, "Yeah, but I won't be."

Rose never bats an eye and goes back to reading her magazine. She was used to stuff like this.

* * *

Ralph Mellanby likes to tell a story. Ralph was the executive producer of *Hockey Night in Canada* back in the eighties. He got an
Emmy for coverage of the 1980 Olympics and the Miracle on Ice.
He was running *Hockey Night in Canada* when I was coaching the
Boston Bruins and Stan Jonathan and Pierre Bouchard had their
fight where Jonathan broke Bouchard's nose and did a real number on him.

I'll tell that story later, but we were all in Boston looking at the
TV to see the replay because in Boston, they'd show replays of
fights. But there was no replay.

We're goin' nuts. We're shouting, "What happened?" and we
find out that *Hockey Night in Canada* was doin' the game and
that *Hockey Night in Canada* didn't show replays of fights.

The next game is back in Montreal and one of my players, who
wasn't really a good fighter, got in a fight with one of their players
and got cut. So as my player come over to see what I wanted to do,
whether I wanted him to go in and get stitched or not, I thought,
"I bet they're playing that one again."

So if you remember in the Montreal Forum, there was a hallway
leading right off the visiting team's bench, and that's where the
Hockey Night in Canada studio was.

I must have been nuts in those days. I ran down the hall while the
game was on, slid by the door a little, and ran into their control
room. There's Ralph sittin' there watchin' the game.

I grabbed him by the shoulder and said, "I suppose you're gonna
show that one."

He says, "No, we don't show replays of fights."

I look up. The player is still bleedin' at the bench, waitin' to see
what to do, the only guy behind the bench is the trainer. And
they're gettin' ready to drop the puck.

So I go out and leave the room with Ralph shakin' his head and
I tell the guy, "Go and get stitched up."

Ralph likes to tell that story. He says it's the strangest thing that ever happened to him in television.

* * *

In every small city, there's always a guy who's handicapped and, I hate to say it, a little slow, a guy that guys make fun of. There was one in Kingston called Teddy. I'm not gonna say his last name.

He kinda jumped along when he walked, and his one arm was by his side and guys made fun of him. In the pool hall, he used to rack up the balls for the guys. That was how he made his money. It was sad to see sometimes with everybody pickin' on him.

But my dad taught me a lesson. It was a pretty good lesson. He didn't mean to. It just happened.

My dad used to get dressed up. You couldn't believe how he'd get dressed up—to the nines. He was six foot two. He'd get made-to-measure suits, vests. The vests were always made tight, and for a guy six foot two, he had a small waist, thirty-two inches. He had a seventeen-and-a-half-inch neck.

On the vest, the chains used to sway. I have a vest too, and they just lay there, but his used to sway. Black mackinaw coat. White silk scarf with *DJC* monogrammed on it with tassels. Tight, tight leather gloves. A Dunhill cigarette holder with Buckingham cigarettes. Dacks shoes. A homburg. Man, he'd stop traffic.

On Saturdays, he'd dress like that on the way downtown. He would get a haircut every week and he'd go down to the RCHA club and on the way down, he'd stop at the pool hall all the time. It was funny to see him in the pool hall dressed like this.

They had one of those statues of Mercury or something. I never went into that pool hall. It was more of an adult one. I used to go into Greer's, and this was Pappas Pool. None of the young kids went into that one. It always had the gaslight going. The statue had this gaslight goin', and I remember lookin' in one time and Dad lit his cigarette on this flame sticking up. He looked super.

He never played pool. He just went in for a short visit, and he used to treat Teddy awful kind all the time. Mr. Pappas told me later that every time Dad would go down, he would always give Teddy a little bit of money—not much, but he'd always buy him chocolate milk and a hot dog and talk to him all the time.

Mr. Pappas used to tell me he was the only guy who treated Teddy like that. It taught me a lesson.

After Dad died, I was sitting there at the wake one night and it was dark. I was sittin' all by myself. It was early, and nobody was in. Nobody could see me. I was sittin' there over in the corner. I was in a daze and my dad was layin' in the coffin.

Teddy come in, shuffling along, hopping along. There was nobody in the building at the time. I don't know what had happened. Usually, there's somebody to greet, but nobody did this time.

Teddy come in. He didn't see me over in the corner. He shook Dad's hand and kissed him.

AL'S NOTE: *Sad to say, Don told me that Teddy was murdered years later.*

* * *

When I went away to play in Barrie for Hap Emms, you must realize that Hap was as cheap as Eddie Shore. I seemed to hit them all.

We actually had equipment that was twenty years old. As I said before, we had to cut old inner tubes to make rubber bands instead of using tape. Gloves were falling apart. This was in the fifties, and we actually had equipment—we should have saved it—that had the names of Dit Clapper and Eddie Shore on it. They'd shipped up all their old equipment, and we were wearing it. It's hard to believe now when I see the kids.

My mother come up and saw me with the gloves I had that were literally falling off. There were holes in them. She went and bought me the most beautiful pair of hockey gloves you ever saw. When Barrie stopped in Oshawa, she came down and gave them to me. I tell ya, it was one of the greatest presents I ever received, and when you look at the pictures in this book, that's the gloves that my mother gave me.

I almost wanted to take them home and sleep with them. All the guys saw my mom give me the gloves. They didn't make fun of me. I know what they thought. They thought that a mother's love is the best of all.

Every time I look at that picture, I think of Maw goin' down and getting those gloves. I loved her all the more.

* * *

I begged Maw to let me buy a Labrador pup and she did. I called it Dudgeon.

I left the next year to play junior hockey in Barrie and left Dudgeon with her.

I selfishly came back with a bulldog from Barrie and left that with Maw as well (as I read this, I think what a jerk I was).

Maw now had to take care of two dogs, and I came home the next year with a budgie called Petey.

The bulldog, Topper, died young, but Dudgeon and Petey were Maw's companions for a long time after Dad died.

Dudgeon loved Maw—they were always together—and Petey was a funny bird. He (or she, I never figured out which) would be on the table when we were playin' cards and he'd be hoppin' around and pickin' up cards and droppin' them off the table to watch them fall.

Every morning, Petey would fly down and sit on Maw's finger and pick at Maw's toast. It was a real treat. Petey lived to be about twelve years old.

One day I got a call from Maw. She was all upset and cryin'. Petey had died.

* * *

I was standing in the studio when Dave Hodge threw his pen, and most people who know *Hockey Night in Canada* know what you're talking about when you say Dave Hodge threw his pen.

Dave Hodge was one of those guys who had his ways, and he would never, ever change them.

They wanted to have one of those games with the Russians and they wanted to have another network do half the game and he would do half the game.

He said, "No. I either do the all the game or I'm not goin' to do any."

Every week they'd come in and say, "Look, this is the way it's going to be," and he'd say, "No. I'm not doin' it."

They even brought in Molson's and they said, "Look, this is the way it's gonna be."

And he said, "No, I either do it all, or I'm not gonna do any."

So he stuck to his guns. He did it all.

AL'S NOTE: *In those days, Molson's owned* Hockey Night in Canada. *They also owned the production company that put it on the air. The show was seen on the CBC, but Molson's paid all the salaries. So when someone from Molson's got involved, his word was usually law.*

* * *

So this one night, we had done our Toronto game. It had finished, and the other game had gone a little longer, and Philadelphia was playin' Montreal.

In the afternoon, CBC—I don't understand curling that well, but they had cut away to show something else when Newfoundland was throwin' their final rock. It was like goin' into overtime, I guess, and they cut away for something political. It was an NDP question-and-answer or somethin'.

So the hockey score is 3–2 and in those days, the news was the main thing. We couldn't cut into the news with Peter Mansfred. That was the big thing. The news started at eleven o'clock.

So we're showin' the Montreal game and gettin' close to the news, and Dave Hodge says to the people in the studio, "Don't come to me if they tie it up, 'cause I'm not gonna tell 'em we're cutting away for the news."

He musta told 'em three times: "Don't come to me. I'm not gonna tell 'em."

Well, sure enough, Scott Mellanby scored the goal to tie it up, and they came to Dave.

He said something to the effect of, "Well, Philadelphia has just tied it up and the game is still goin', but we've got to cut away for the news. That's the way they do it around the CBC."

And he flipped his pen.

I knew. He knew and I knew that was the end. But that's the way he was.

He had his ways and he would not change. He was right, too, by the way. They cut into the news now like they should have back then.

AL'S NOTE: *The NDP is the New Democratic Party. They're left wingers, so naturally, they don't get a lot of support from Don. Peter Mansfred is actually Peter Mansbridge, the CBC news anchor. But Don always calls him Mansfred.*

* * *

They went after Dave Hodge and said, "Look, just apologize. Just say you're sorry and you'll come back. Just say you were wrong."

He says, "I'm not goin' to say I was wrong, 'cause I wasn't wrong." So away goes Dave after fourteen or fifteen years.

I had no idea who was comin' in. Some guy from out west, and in he comes. He looked to be about nineteen years old, and of course it was Ron MacLean.

I had heard that he was a weatherman and did some sports on TV. John Shannon saw him and hired him. He had big shoes to fill. Hodge had been with the CBC sixteen years.

I remember the first time I met MacLean. I was sitting on the set of *Hockey Night in Canada* and in he walks and says, "I'm Ron MacLean," just before we went on.

I said, "Don't be nervous, kid. There's only two million people watching."

* * *

I would like to say we clicked right off the bat, but we didn't.

Evidently, he'd had a habit of looking down during an interview, and they told him to stop it. So during our first interview, he was concentrating so hard on not looking down that tears come into his eyes. I look over and his left eye had the biggest tear you ever saw.

I thought, "Is this guy goin' to tear up every time we do 'Coach's Corner'?"

* * *

Also, he was getting advice from everybody on how to handle me. For instance, I learned later that Hodge told him, "The only advice I'm going to give you is don't let him pick the topics."

That's 'cause Hodge wouldn't let me pick the topics. One time, the first game of the 1984 Stanley Cup final between the Islanders and Oilers, I went to the morning skate and I really liked the looks of a kid they'd got from the Pittsburgh Penguins, Kevin McClelland.

I said to Hodge, "Ask me about this kid McClelland, will you? I have a good feelin' about him."

He didn't. The score was 1–0 that night and McClelland scored the goal.

* * *

I remember I was playin' in Rochester and I had the strangest fight I was ever in. I can't remember his name, but he had long black hair and no helmet. So we're in the fight and I had him sort of by the throat, and I hit him and he went down on his knees.

As he went down, my left thumb went in his mouth and went over to the side. He clamped down on my thumb and he had his molars in there, and he was actually trying to bite off my thumb.

I hit him, but it didn't do any good. The harder I hit him, the more he bit down on my thumb.

Well, I tell ya, you talk about panic. I could see the blood comin' out of his mouth and it was my blood from my thumb. I still have the scar. I really believe he was trying to bite my thumb off, and he was doin' a pretty good job.

So I figure I gotta get my thumb out of his mouth. If I don't, he's gonna have it off. I've got to bite the bullet and pull my thumb out of his mouth.

So I grab him by the hair and give him a good shot to get his mind off my thumb and pull as hard as I can and lo and behold, he has no teeth in the front. Oh joy. Oh joy. Let me tell you somethin'. He really paid for bitin' my thumb.

Ever have a guy try to bite your thumb off? Course not. What a feeling that was, because the harder I hit him, the harder he bit. I tell you one thing, I never ever put my thumb in a guy's mouth again.

That was the strangest fight I was ever in.

I've still got the scar.

* * *

I have often been asked by people trying to break into TV how I've lasted more than 20 years. I really don't know what to tell 'em because I'm not really a TV guy.

I don't think. I just react. Ron MacLean does all the thinking.

I told you before how he can re-do a five-minute piece and repeat the original version word for word.

Sometimes people come on the set to meet us—sponsors or CBC guests and so on—and while Ron's in conversation with these people, the director will say in his earpiece, "Boston just scored in the other game. Give us an update."

Ron will ask, "Who scored? Any assists?" Then, without having seen the highlight before, he'll describe the goal when they're showing it.

Then he'll turn back to the people on the set and carry on the conversation without missing a beat.

I could never do that. Like I said, I don't think, I just react.

One time when I was in junior, we were having a team meeting and Hap Emms was the coach. I said, "I think we should do it this way, Hap."

He said, "Don't think Don. You'll only hurt the club."

So I tell people I have no idea why I have lasted this long. I don't really want to find out because if I ever do find out why I've lasted this long, I'd probably screw it up.

* * *

At the start, I must admit, MacLean was not my cup of tea. He was a team player, which I am not. For instance, I found out in one game that Guy Lafleur, in the first period, had broke his ankle, and I was gonna put it on "Coach's Corner."

He said, "Oh no, we must share that with the fellows up above."

Needless to say, I had something to say to him about that. We got that business straightened out in a hurry.

I said I wasn't a team guy, but I have to tell you why I'm not a team guy.

Ron could never understand that at the start. Besides history books, I read a lot of books. I've read every story about every movie star there is, and I've read all about the producers and directors—

Cecil B. DeMille, Howard Hughes, Sam Goldwyn, Louis B. Mayer. I've read all their life stories.

There were two that really fascinated me: Bette Davis and Joan Crawford. Now, they were back in the thirties when men ran all the studios. They ran everything. Bette Davis found that she had to be tough and Joan Crawford had to be tough.

In this industry, they called them monsters. One day, Bette Davis explained that.

She said, "Look, when the picture is a failure, who do they put up? Do they say it's the producer's failure? The director's failure? No. They say it's a Bette Davis failure."

I found it the same way on television. If somethin' goes wrong with the show, they never give it to the producers or directors. They just give me heck. I was the guy, so if I'm gonna get it. I'm gonna take it myself.

I didn't mind that in hockey. I didn't mind a guy that wanted to score a goal that had his mind like that.

I think of Alex Ovechkin. When he gets the puck, he doesn't care. He's not passing the puck. He's gonna put it in. A lot of people would say he's selfish, but if he wasn't selfish, he wouldn't get all those goals.

Gretzky got 139 goals in a weekend tournament when he was a kid. How many times do you think *he* passed the puck?

Anyhow, that was my theory. I'm thinkin' of "Coach's Corner" and "Coach's Corner" only. To do it the other way, I wish them good luck. That's the way it is.

* * *

At the start Ron did not appreciate my wise-guy attitude. One time I told him I was going to say something about a player and he said, "You can't say that. Think of his mother."

So things were not going well until one morning after a skate in Calgary. It was a nice day and we walked all the way back to the hotel and got things straightened out.

The night before, I had kidded him on "Coach's Corner" that he should wear a red cowboy hat like I was wearing because he was cheering for Calgary so much.

He went nuts and he was hurt. He just didn't understand at the time that he had to be ready for anything on "Coach's Corner," so after that, he started giving it back to me.

Now he's better at giving me the gears than I am at giving him the gears.

* * *

Ron MacLean can put the pops away with the best, but he is really a wine guy with hundreds of bottles of wine in his cellar. He owns a sailboat that's in the Caribbean. He has partners. In other words, he travels in different circles than me.

He is a semi-tree-hugger. He believes in a lot of left-wing ideas.

When we walk through airports, people will holler, "Great show, Don," and say nothing to him. He just laughs.

People will ask for my autograph and not his, and my picture and not his. He really sincerely thinks it's funny.

One time, a guy wanted to take a picture of me with his wife. Ron went to step into the picture and the guy hollered, "Get out! You're ruining the picture!"

Ron got the biggest kick out of that. I don't think I could handle it the way he does but he has so much confidence in himself that it doesn't bother him.

* * *

His memory is incredible. When we did *Hockey Day in Canada* in Winkler, Manitoba, this kid had given me a tie. Two months later, I wanted to name the kid on TV. I said, "Do you remember the name of the kid that gave me the tie?"

No hesitation. "Yeah, it was Brian Whitehead."

It was a kid he met in the crowd and remembered his name!

Name any player and MacLean knows where he came from, his number, his record, where he was drafted. Sometimes he makes me feel like a dummy. (Don't say it.)

Looking at us, I look like a redneck and he looks like an intellectual. The strangest thing is that he reads nothing but sports books. I read some sports books, but mostly I'm into history and biographies of famous leaders like Lord Horatio Nelson and Lawrence of Arabia. Sir Francis Drake.

* * *

When Ron almost lost his job a few years back, everybody thinks it was for a lot of money. Believe it or not, it was over $25,000, which I know is a fair sum, but to lose a job like his over it doesn't make sense.

It did to him.

I don't know the exact circumstances. It was promises or somethin', but they were not comin' through, so he was quitting over it and it leaked out.

Once that happened, there were more than 12,500 emails about it, so the CBC talked to him again and they changed their mind. But he was ready to pack it in for $25,000 because of a promise.

* * *

The guy is a nut with tips. I'm not bad, but he tips sometimes 50 percent. His motto is that everybody has got to live.

When we're travelling and people stop us for an autograph and picture—again, I'm not bad, but he goes into, "How are you? Where are you travelling to? Where do you live? How many children do you have?" and all that stuff. He gets their life story.

And the first thing you know, they're talkin' about families and everything.

I'm saying, "Come on, we gotta get goin'." But he's like that.

* * *

He's a real team player and is always helping people out. I'm not.

He never had to grind it out. He was successful from the word go. When he was young, he started out as an announcer on radio with music. He started to do sports, then the news. He ended up running the station. Then he came onto TV.

Shannon picked him up as a kid and handed him the plum job at *Hockey Night in Canada.* He is a rarity—successful from the word go.

In some ways, he reminds me of Hodge. Hodge could do a segment, and if they told him to do it over, he'd do it over and never miss a word. MacLean's the same way. If Hodge felt he didn't want to do something, you couldn't move him. MacLean is the same way. They both have principles.

I, on the other hand, lived with the sharks. I've been unemployed, scratching for a living with guys after your blood, bosses calling you "reprehensible" and "despicable" in the paper, telling you it's your last year, thousands of people looking for you to fail.

I've had to live by my wits and I'm sorry to say that sometimes I've been devious. I've been in a position where I was drowning and got thrown an anchor, but survived anyway.

If someone had to go over the side of the ship so I could survive, over they went. No mercy. Very few people showed me mercy.

Hey, I realize I put myself in these positions—quitting school, not learning a trade. I'm not whining or complaining. I'm just telling you how I had to fight. When you're down and out, you do anything to survive. I know I don't sound like a very nice person, but don't judge a man until you've walked in his moccasins.

I'm doing okay now and I'm enjoying every minute, but never a day goes by that I don't remember how miserable I was and the humiliation of not having a job.

I remember well the hurting, and nobody had better ever try to be responsible for having me go back to those dark days again.

I'm aware and tuned. I really don't have many talents—in school, in hockey or on TV—but I have one talent and I have never been wrong: I can meet a person for five seconds and know what they think of me and their angle. I had to be able to do that to survive.

I just read this over. I really got carried away here, and some people would think that I'm layin' on a little thick. But I'm betting there's a lot of people who know the awful feeling of not getting a job. Whether it's real or imagined, you think people see you as a failure, and let me say it again. If I get the feeling some person might be the cause of me going back to those days, let's just say they'd better be ready.

* * *

Throughout the summer of 2008, people were asking me what I thought about the CBC losing the rights to the *Hockey Night in Canada* theme.

I have to tell ya, I love the song and I wish we still had it. I guess the other people offered more money. If it's true that they got $2.5 million, that's a lot of money and everybody has their price.

I kinda related it to me in a way. I've been with the CBC for over twenty years and the song has been with us for over forty years.

I must admit my twenty years have been a rocky ride sometimes, what with the seven-second delay and things like that. One boss—who is now gone by the way—called me "reprehensible" and "despicable."

A lot of people probably didn't know until they read it in this book that a few years ago, I was told by another boss that I was going into my last season. She's gone too.

As I said before, I think she thought I'd quit, but I just bided my time.

My years on *Hockey Night in Canada* have been a lot of fun, but at times, no bed of roses. I will admit now that I was thinking of leaving *Hockey Night in Canada*.

I was offered more money and a longer contract, and when some-one explained to me what "reprehensible" and "despicable" meant, I thought I would grab the money and run, like the people who own the song did.

But I got to thinking, the only reason the other company wants me was that I was—and am—on *Hockey Night in Canada*. If I hadn't made *Hockey Night in Canada* and become semi-famous, they wouldn't want me.

In my opinion, this song is in the same situation. The song would be nothin' if it wasn't on *Hockey Night in Canada*.

Sure I love it, and everybody loves it. But I love it because it was on *Hockey Night in Canada*.

It's just like me. If I wasn't on *Hockey Night in Canada*, I'd just be another broken-down hockey player. In my opinion, without the song being on *Hockey Night in Canada*, it would be just another jingle.

* * *

I was asked if I ever regretted saying anything on TV. One thing, it was in the Chicago–Edmonton series in 1990. I was on with Dave Hodge and Randy Gregg, defenseman for Edmonton. He is also a doctor. Randy had a breakaway and really looked bad not scoring, and I said, "How would you like that guy operating on your heart?"

My mother phoned me the next day and really ripped me. "It's okay to talk about hockey but when you get personal, that's wrong."

Mom was right, as usual. I was wrong.

* * *

I'm often asked "How did *Grapeline* get started?" That's the radio show I do with Brian Williams, and the guy who got it going was my friend Gerry Patterson.

I had done a commercial for Bridgestone tires and Gerry said, "Let's try and see if Bridgestone will sponsor a radio show."

Gerry saw the head of Bridgestone, Herb Stein, and got a cheque, and then went down to CFRB radio in Toronto and met Prior Smith.

Prior Smith said, "Yes, what can I do for you?"

Gerry said, "I would like to start a radio show with Don Cherry involved."

Prior said, "Do you know how many people would like to start and have a radio show? The line is a mile long."

Gerry said, "Yes, I understand that. Would this speed up the procedure?"

He opened his briefcase and handed Prior a cheque for $100,000 for a show with Bridgestone as a sponsor.

Prior said, "When do you want to start? Tomorrow?"

That was how the show got started with Brian Williams. That was twenty-four years ago.

Brian likes to tell everybody that when we started, I said to him, "Do you think I have enough stories to go for a whole year?"

I guess I did.

* * *

I got in trouble a lot with Mr. Campbell. He had been at the Nuremberg trials. He was a lawyer. He was a very stern person.

Everybody called him *Mr.* Campbell. It was never, "Campbell" or "Clarence." Even his enemies called him Mr. Campbell.

In Pittsburgh, to this day, the coach has to go across the ice to get from the bench to the dressing room. This time, I'm mad at the referee, Ron Wicks, and as I'm going across the ice, I start goin' fast so I can catch up to him.

I slide and I bang into him and I hit him against the glass. I didn't mean to do it, but now I'm in deep trouble.

I've already been in trouble because Mr. Campbell feels the

Bruins are too aggressive and fighting too much—the whole deal. He told me, "Keep your team under control and stop saying smart things to the press all the time."

He had already fined me $2000. Two thousand dollars! That's a lot of money. I was only makin' $40,000 at the time.

So I'm in Buffalo and John Wensink gets in a fight with, of all guys, Ric Seiling.

Ric Seiling! So Ric Seiling turtles and John did the only thing he could do. He bit him on the back.

He really did! Seiling had to go for tetanus shots, the whole thing.

Now, I've already been told to keep the team under control and not say things to the press.

Dick Johnson, the writer for the Buffalo paper, comes runnin' in afterwards and says, "There, Cherry! What do you think of John Wensink biting Ric Seiling?"

I says, "That's what I like—hungry hockey players."

* * *

Mr. Campbell is really mad at me for that, and then I do this thing with Wicks. Now I know I'm really in trouble because I've banged a referee.

Sure enough, Dale Hamilton, the Bruins' secretary and Harry's right hand, says, "Don, you'd better phone Mr. Campbell. He wants to speak to you."

You're always afraid to phone Mr. Campbell because he just terrifies everybody, but I phone and say, "Hello, this is Don Cherry."

"Mr. Campbell will be with you in a minute."

That's how they did it. He always kept you waitin' a few minutes, and this is how he answered the phone: "Campbell here. Explain your actions in Pittsburgh."

I says, "Well, Mr. Campbell, I didn't mean to. I went on the ice and I didn't mean to slide. I slid."

He says, "That's the most feeble, insipid excuse I've ever heard in my life," and he just ripped me to shreds and he fined me another two grand!

The way this is goin', by the end of the season, I'm going to end up *owing* money.

* * *

So now it's in Montreal in the summer and he's very old now. Back then, the annual NHL congress was a terrific thing. I don't know why they don't do it now. They got a great big room at the Queen Elizabeth Hotel and all the important people, the general managers and governors, sat at a long table in the middle.

All the coaches and floaters and everybody else sat around the room along the wall. There had to be about sixty people sat around the room. It was really interesting. The coaches could go there and sit there. You never said a word 'cause you'd get thrown out. There was no jerkin' around. You just sat there and listened.

Mr. Campbell called a time out. He had to go to the washroom 'cause he was gettin' old.

There was silence when he stood up. He was like the king! And he started to walk along, shuffled actually, lookin' straight ahead. We're all sittin' there lookin', and halfway down the line, he stopped and looked at me for a second and slowly put out his hand and said, "How are you, young man?"

I rose slowly, almost wanting to bow. I kid you not. And I said, "Fine thanks, Mr. Campbell."

Mr Campbell nodded and turned and continued on slowly. Nobody said a word until he left the room. Complete silence. All eyes came back to me, and I know what they were thinking: why would Mr. Campbell stop and only acknowledge me, who caused him so much trouble? I could never figure that one out myself.

* * *

I attend many minor hockey games with my son, Tim. Tim is an OHL scout for Central Scouting, and I see a lot of hockey parents. They are the best. Hockey is an expensive sport and they sacrifice money and time for their young players. But every once in a while I see a young boy run out and say to his dad after the game, "Dad, Dad, did you see me score that goal?" all excited and happy. And the father says, "You should have scored three." And the kid's face drops. Why do some parents do this? Encourage, encourage, encourage. Anybody can criticize.

I remember when I was fifteen, the head of the Boston Bruins scouts, Harold "Baldy" Cotton, was comin' to see me play in Kingston. I was so nervous I played the worst game of my life.

Hockey meant so much to me and I remember walking home from the arena with tears in my eyes. My big chance gone, I'm the lowest of low. I walk into my dad's bedroom, sit sown on the side of the bed, and I say, "I guess I blew it, eh, Dad?"

I can still see him now. He always read in bed with his glasses on his nose. I remember him saying, "Oh I don't know, what about the time you blocked that shot? And what about the time you took that guy out?" And proceeded to tell me the few good things I did in that game.

I can honestly tell you I was so pumped when I left that bedroom I could hardly wait for the next game.

I was back to positive again.

* * *

One regret I have in life was that Dad would get *The Hockey News* and there was never anything written about the American Hockey League.

Sometimes it would have a puzzle: "Two brothers are named Dick and Don. What is their last name?"

Dad would get to the little part in the summary where I'd get a penalty and he'd cut that out because there was never any stories written, just the summaries.

I often think now how happy he would have been to see that at least I get my name in the paper and on television.

But at the time he died—it was 1962—I was the lowest of the low. I'd turned into—and I hate to say it, it hurts me to say it—a hockey bum. I was goin' from here to there. I was goin' to Kitchener. I was goin' to Three Rivers. I was goin' to Springfield. I was goin' to Spokane. I was goin' all over the place.

He still thought the world of me and he always thought I was goin' to make it to the National Hockey League.

He said, "You'll make it someday. Keep goin'."

And I guess in a way, he was right. I did make it to the National Hockey League—not in the way he was thinking of it, and maybe looking down now he's proud of me.

I don't think he was too proud of me when he died. I know he loved me, but I don't think he was too proud. How could he be?

Maybe he's lookin' down now and he's a little proud.

IN MEMORY OF OUR FALLEN SOLDIERS

Fallen soldier Capt. Matthew Dawe of C Company Princess Pats
with his son, Lucas, just before his deployment to Afghanistan.

God bless all our brave soldiers.

INDEX

CAREER HIGHLIGHTS

PLAYING
- Won the Memorial Cup with the Barrie Flyers 1952–53
- Played seventeen years as a pro: 102 goals, 265 assists, 1345 PIM
- Won four Calder Cups in the American Hockey League
- Won a Western League Championship with the Vancouver Canucks

COACHING
- Coach of Pittsford High in Rochester, New York: championship, undefeated season v playoffs
- Coach and general manager of Rochester Americans, twice named Coach of the Year in the American Hockey League
- Coach of the Boston Bruins for five years
- NHL Coach of the Year
- Coach of the Colorado Rockies
- Owner and coach of the Mississauga Ice Dogs
- Assistant Coach with Team Canada, won the Canada Cup in 1976
- Head Coach of Team Canada at the World Championships in Sweden in 1981
- Coach of Team Cherry for Ontario Hockey League Prospects Games

My biggest thrill in hockey? That I could stand back of the Boston bench and watch Bobby Orr. Bobby Clarke said, "Bobby Orr is so good that there should be a higher league he can play in." But I think Serge Savard said it best, "There's players, stars, superstars, and then there's Bobby Orr." He was so right.

PHOTO CREDITS

Every effort has been made to contact copyright holders. In the event of omission or error, the publisher should be notified at Doubleday Canada, 1 Toronto Street, Suite 300, Toronto, ON, Canada M5C 2V6.

INSERT ONE
Page iv (top and bottom) © Steve Babineau/NHLI via Getty Images

INSERT TWO
Page ii (top) © Bruce Bennett Studios/Getty Images;
Page v © Boston Globe/Frank O'Brien/Landov

INSERT THREE
Page i (top) © Dave Sanford/Getty Images; (bottom left) © Darren Makowichuk, Sun Media Corp; (bottom right) © Michael Peake, Sun Media Corp.
Page ii (top) © Malcolm Mayes/artizans.com; (bottom) © Boston Globe/Chris Wattie/Landov
Page iii (bottom) © Dave Sanford/Getty Images/NHLI
Page iv courtesy of Toronto Star Archives
Page vi (top left and bottom) © Jeff Vinnick/Getty Images
Page vii (top) © Chris Relke/Getty Images; (bottom) © Phillip MacCallum/Getty Images for NHL

INTERIOR
Page 223 © Darryl Dyck, Sun Media Corp.

All other photos courtesy of the author.